ALSO BY GUCCI MANE

The Autobiography of Gucci Mane

The Gucci Mane Guide to Greatness

GUCCI MANE WITH SOREN BAKER

SIMON & SCHUSTER

NEW YORK   LONDON   TORONTO   SYDNEY   NEW DELHI

Simon & Schuster
1230 Avenue of the Americas
New York, NY 10020

First Simon & Schuster hardcover edition October 2020

SIMON & SCHUSTER and colophon are registered trademarks
of Simon & Schuster, Inc.

For information about special discounts for bulk purchases,
please contact Simon & Schuster Special Sales at 1-866-506-1949
or business@simonandschuster.com.

The Simon & Schuster Speakers Bureau can bring authors
to your live event. For more information or to book an event,
contact the Simon & Schuster Speakers Bureau at 1-866-248-3049
or visit our website at www.simonspeakers.com.

Interior design by Carly Loman

Manufactured in the United States of America

3   5   7   9   10   8   6   4   2

Library of Congress Control Number: 2020940379

ISBN 978-1-9821-4678-8
ISBN 978-1-9821-4680-1 (ebook)

To the memory of my mother and father

Intro

xiii

We Got a Long Way to Go! xv

Part I
The Essentials

1

Stop Underestimating Yourself 3 | It's Imperative That I Change the Narrative 7 | Time Is Valuable, Spend It Wisely 11 | Refocus and Go Harder 19 | Just Keep Improving 25 | Do What You Got to Do 31 | Find Something to Be 35

Part II
The Process

41

Every Day Is a Chance to Get Better 43 | Look Up, Look Down, Then Look Around 47 | Embrace Every Challenge 51 | Work in Silence 55 | Be Resilient 59

Part III
Accountability 101

67

Everybody Must Be Held Accountable 69 | Self-Discipline Brings Riches 75 | Self-Awareness Is a Valuable Weapon 81

Part IV
Your People   87

Choose Your Friends Carefully 89 | Avoid Lazy and Miserable
People 95 | Haters Are Going to Say You Were Cloned 99 |
Women Are Brilliant 103 | If You Don't Know the Old Me, You Don't
Really Know Me 107 | Protect Yourself at All Times 111 |
Never Let Being Liked Get in the Way of Being Respected 117 |
Lead by Example 121

Part V
Work Ethic   125

Nobody Cares. Work Harder 127 | Don't Be Lazy 131 | When They
Sleep, I'm Grinding 135 | Do More, Get More 139 | Whatever It Is,
Do It Now 143

Part VI
Opportunity   145

Stay Ready 147 | I Can Make Something Outta Nothin' 149 | Make
Today Count 153 | I Turn Burdens into Blessings 159

Part VII
Success
165

Whatever You're Thinking, Think Bigger 167 | I'm Cut from a Different Cloth 171 | Prepare Yourself to Be Successful 177 | Relax, but Don't Get Comfortable 183 | I Don't Do Things for Fun 189 | Learn to Compartmentalize 195 | Fuck Everybody, Stack Your Bread 199

Part VIII
The Power of Love
203

I Love My Wife 205 | I Told My Wife Her Presence Is the Present 211 | Livin' the Life, Me and My Fine-Ass Wife 215 | Hot Wife, Rich Husband 219 | I'd Rather Just Chill Wit' Babe 227 | Happy Wife, Happy Life 229

Part IX
Final Words
231

I'm Blessed and Grateful 233 | If You Keep Looking Back, You'll Trip Going Forward 237 | Never Quit on Yourself! 239

Acknowledgments 241
Photo Credits 245

Intro

We Got a Long Way to Go!

This book is powerful. The words you are about to read can help you. That's because there is truth in them. These are words of wisdom, like the Bible and its proverbs. Why does the Bible give people strength? Because the Bible is a book of words filled with truth. This book describes a path—the ongoing path to greatness.

I wanted to write this book to give you a tool set. It's not an autobiography. I already did that. I'm doing this book because I really feel like it can help people. I live by the principles in this book. I'm serious with it.

I want to reach people. I know how they think. This book should touch people who are going through something. This is my way to teach them. It's not going to be easy. But study these words, and put them into action. Start now.

This is my way to get my message out even further. I know people liked *The Autobiography of Gucci Mane*. There were lessons to be learned from the story of my life. But I've got even more to reveal. When you get this book, you'll see it's a visual book that you can flip though. You'll see that my body changed. I used to be fat. Now I'm skinny. Man, now I'm married. You can look at the good things, the bad things. There are so many things that are eye-grabbing. Study it all, then it totally makes sense. I stand on all this.

I hope this book brings a little solace to everybody. That's what we're trying to get to. But we got a long way to go. I hope these little words of wisdom will help you get through your day. I want this book to be something where you keep going to it. You can put it on your shelf and keep going to *The Gucci Mane Guide to Greatness*.

I want this book to keep you motivated and make you say, "Damn, man. This stuff right here, it does make sense. I've seen how he did it. Even though I read this book once, I'm going to read it again. I can read it in two or three days. I'm going to keep coming back to it for guidance and inspiration."

Since I got in the music game, I've given everyone a lot of insight into my life. It's been a wild journey, that's for sure. I was born in Alabama and became a man in Georgia. My daddy taught me how to read people. I learned the streets by being in them. I robbed people, sold drugs, then became a fiend myself. I liked rap, but didn't like the way my voice sounded. I always imagined myself as the CEO, the man investing in the talent. I always liked the CEO better than the rapper anyway.

Then I realized that people loved me. That made me understand I could be both—the CEO *and* the rapper. People loved my raps, but they loved me in person, too. They loved talking to me, getting advice from me, hearing what I had to say. Here I was, a kid from Alabama commanding the respect of everyone in Atlanta. Then Georgia. Then the South. Then the rap world. Now, I've done songs with Bruno Mars, Drake, Migos, Rae Sremmurd, Selena Gomez,

Chris Brown, Fifth Harmony, Mariah Carey, Justin Bieber, 2 Chainz, Nicki Minaj—the list goes on. I've helped raise a new generation of Atlanta talent. I brought trap to the masses.

When you see me today, I'm a much different man than I was when I got in the game. Actually, I'm much different than I was even two or three years ago. I'm about half the man I was. Literally. I've lost more than a hundred pounds. I don't do any drugs. I don't drink. I work out all the time. I'm married now. I'm reading books, thinking differently. I'm in a whole different mindset now. Now I can take in more knowledge.

Look at the results. I make an impression. My singles regularly go platinum. I've got millions and millions of followers on social media. I act. My memoir, *The Autobiography of Gucci Mane*, was a *New York Times* bestseller. I'm more popular now than I've ever been. And I won't stop.

I'm still young. But I've lived a life. I love my life. I've gained a lot of wisdom through the years. The last time I was in prison I made a choice. I would hold myself accountable, and change my life so I could handle life straight up. I have established principles that guide me every day. I've benefited from them so much that I wanted to share them with the world, so that others can benefit from what I've learned. My whole idea with this book is that everyone should take advantage of their own natural ability and drive to be success-ful. My grind has helped lead to my success. This is the path I'm walking every day. This is what makes me get the most out of my twenty-four hours.

People look at me as a role model, for the good I'm doing, so I decided to write a book of affirmations of sorts. It's a collection of inspirational "Guccisms," you could say. I partnered with respected rap journalist and fellow author Soren Baker to give you my *Guide to Greatness*. We built upon my pronouncements to give you all a playbook for success. Here is most everything I've learned over the years.

The Gucci Mane Guide to Greatness is a self-help book. At the same time, it's coming off my autobiography, so there's a little bit of a Part II in here, too. *The Autobiography of Gucci Mane* covered everything from my birth until the day I got out of jail. But a lot has changed since then. I'm a whole new man. I want people to look at what I've done and see: "This is how he got there."

Make no mistake, I still mess up all the time. Life isn't easy and we all have a long way to go if we really, truly want to be the best we can be. Life is brutal. It's highly competitive. Everyone has to grind to get there. Every day. So whether you grew up in the trap, or only heard about it through my music or saw it in one of my videos, it doesn't matter.

This book is a challenge. It's *The Gucci Mane Guide to Greatness*. Don't underestimate yourself. Don't think that what you're saying is not important. Don't think you can't achieve the impossible. I want this book to inspire people. Everyone needs some game, so here it is. *The Gucci Mane Guide to Greatness* is for the world. Enjoy.

Part I

The Essentials

Stop Underestimating Yourself

Since I was a child, I've been falling down and getting back up. I've been practicing resilience my whole life. When you're down, it's easy to start underestimating yourself, to let self-doubt creep in, to look at other people and compare yourself. Stop.

If they can do it, you can. That's how I feel about myself. I knew that if I dedicated myself to being a major player in rap, I would. I knew that if I dedicated myself to losing weight and staying in shape, I would. But I had doubts along the way, of course. I was nearly three hundred pounds and I was locked up. Most people probably wouldn't think that's the best place to get in shape. But I knew I could do it, and at least start that process.

It's been an eye-opening shift in how I think. You know how sometimes you're like,

3

"Man, I kind of felt like that person wasn't right, but you know, he's kind of got a lot of hype about him." I used to underestimate myself and overestimate my opponent, my enemy, my rival. It's because you don't know them. That makes it easier to project something positive onto them. It's like they're an alien country, that they're way ahead of you and there's no way you could be on their level.

Let's say I'm building a production company. I'm like, "Live Nation's got all these resources and I don't have any, so there isn't a reason for me to try to make Gucci Nation." No. Don't underestimate yourself. I know a lot of artists. I can be hands-on. I've got a rolodex. That's an advantage. I've got years of experience. That's an advantage. I had to remind myself. Because even if you have fewer people, you're more mobile. So don't complain. Don't underestimate yourself. Whatever you've got, you have enough.

People don't care how you do it. They just want to see results. Nobody knows if you made your album in your room. If it's dope, it's dope. You don't have to record at the Hit Factory or go to Patchwerk for it to be good. Don't underestimate yourself. You can make the beat, record the shit on your computer. You can do it. "You don't have to be Malcolm Gladwell, Gucci. You can write the book your damn self." Here it is. Don't underestimate yourself into thinking like you need somebody to do it. Try to do that shit yourself. You can write the screenplay. You can act in the movie. You can direct the movie. It doesn't matter if you never tried it.

If they can do it, you can. This realization, it never just "clicked" for me like things do for other people. It's just a gradual thing that you practice. It's not a light-bulb "aha" moment. You just have to keep trying. When you start trying, you find out who you are.

Don't underestimate yourself. Whatever you've got, you have enough.

You may grow up admiring someone. Then you work hard and ten years later, you find yourself working with them, not for them. You got there because you deserved it. You belong there. You made it happen. Now you're with your idols handling business.

You either practice quitting or you practice winning. Everyone's going to fail at some point, so which one are you going to be? Are you going to be somebody who's faking, not going hard, and making excuses? Or are you going to be the person who's aware, who's practicing and pushing yourself to do what's right no matter what it is? I now know who I am and what I want to do. So stop underestimating yourself and just do it.

It's Imperative That I Change the Narrative

We are the authors of our lives. We are the writers of our own stories. We have the power to say who we are and what we want to be. The story you tell yourself sets the course of the life you live. It creates the road map for what is possible. If you don't like the story you're living, you have the power to change the narrative. That's what authors do. They write stories. They create the plot. Create your own plot.

You've always got another chance, no matter what happens. If you fight through your challenges and your problems, you can overcome them. If you don't fight them, they get worse. If I'm in debt, I don't just quit. I've got to get a job to pay my debtors off a little bit at a time. It might take eight years to pay it off. Are you going to spend eight years in that same job, being grateful that you've got that job? Instead of being like, "Damn. I'm fucked up. I'm a slave to the job."?

In your mind, you've got to be like, "I'm not a slave to nothing. If I don't like this job, I can get another one, or quit." Or, "If I'm smart enough, I'm gonna keep this until I've got something else going." You change the narrative.

A man working eight years works every day Monday through Friday. He's got holidays and some vacation time, when he can get some rest. But everybody's not going to do that. Especially if you're a rapper. That's not a life a rapper wants to live. I turned forty this year. A lot of people are like, "I'm forty-three, forty-four." But they're still immature and they still think it's 2003. That's not the situation you want to be in. You've got to stay in front of it. Once you're popping, you've got to stay in front of it.

It's easy to lose, even when you get it. The stuff with Kobe, he was such a hard worker. I was thinking like, "Damn. Tiger Woods lost so much, but he did it to himself with the distractions. Kobe got distracted, too." You're talking about one of the most acclaimed golfers, one of the most acclaimed basketball players. It's no coincidence that they were friends. They go so hard and are so accomplished, but at the same time, things have been taken from them. Tiger lost his wife. That damn near broke him. He's still kind of a shell of what he was. Kobe, we celebrate him and now he won't be able to be with his wife. But at least he had his wife and his wife stayed down with him during his struggles, so now everything's going to go to her.

Everything can be taken away. It reminds me to humble myself every day. I have been in the same downward spiral, so I can identify with Antonio Brown, with Tiger, with Kobe, dealing with the public humiliation of doing some shit, and it's like, "Damn." It's almost like you forgot to stand in front of your business. You're not appreciating the opportunity that you had and you're not thinking that you can lose it.

Know that you've always got another chance. If you don't like the story you're living, change the narrative.

Time Is Valuable, Spend It Wisely

Really the only thing that you have in the world is time. That's all you got.

If you look at your finances, your health, your mentality, and look at it like a businessperson, you should be able to see if your business is growing or not. Last year, I was in investing mode. I knew my business could lose money the first year. Second year, I'm breaking even. Third year, I'm doing well. If I'm out there just drinking beer and I'm twenty-seven and popular, two years from now, am I popular? Is my career going down? Is my health going down?

If the answer is yes, I know I'm not doing well with my time. And if you're on drugs, you really won't be able to tell. But if you're a lawyer, you can say, "I was spending too much time wining and dining clients instead of working for the ones I already have. That's why things didn't pan out last year. Now I'm in the red."

You've got to be able to judge yourself. Some people get there quicker than other people. It took me a long time to get to the point where I was mature enough to say, "Hey. This is what's going on with me. Let me deal with this right here." It's going to be a long process, no matter what it is, whether it's your finances, or learning how to play an instrument. If I'm starting a record company, I might bump my head a few times before I find the right artist. But you've got to approach it with a positive attitude. I'm going to fix what I did wrong and not be irresponsible and not play games. I know my timeline, and I know that things take time. I didn't always spend my time wisely. This is a lesson I discovered over the course of my life. As I got older, I learned to practice it more effectively.

I had to be a CEO, and not just a part of the record company. I wanted to sit in an executive chair, not just spend some time with or do a song with the artists that I signed. I want to be a part of everything that comes through the company. Now I've got testimonies and I can talk to other artists and it can benefit them. I'm thinking about how I can be helpful, and it's not all about the money. I used to be like, "I'm going to sign them so I can make some money." Now, it's like, "Peep the mistakes that I made."

My time is valuable. I spend it wisely. I give my time to my artists. They know that. I feel like I'm not preaching to them and I'm not a hypocrite. That took time. It took time for me to show myself and the world that I really mean what I say, but at the same time, I'm a work in progress. I'm still doing it and I'm still not where I want to be, but that's why I always try to talk to myself. Now I'm putting it out there to the world, too.

That's why those self-talks are so important. If not, you could go months and months without doing anything. Let's say you put your all into a book and you put it out and people say, "This book is trash," but you know the time you put in by yourself. Or, if you rushed it, you know the time you didn't put in.

So if the book does well and you didn't put any time into it, you think that's how it goes. Don't become stagnant. Don't take your time for granted. If you just keeping working and growing, it's not even about the acclaim. It's almost a numbers thing. That's where I'm at now. What did you do with your 2020? What did you do with your 2021? Okay. How are you going to use all the shit you did in 2005 to 2019 to help you in 2020 and 2021 and 2031?

Maybe now you could do a podcast. Maybe you could be an actor on a reality show because making an album ain't making you any money. But you've still got to approach that podcast or whatever your next step is like you want to make some money. I'm forty, so with years and experience, I feel like I should be able to say, "Hey, man. With the ability and time I've got, I'm going to do what I can do with it, or I'm going to suffer my fate."

So you shouldn't worry about how I spent my time. Don't ask me how long it takes to make a mixtape, or how long I've been in the studio. Did you like the songs that I made? I didn't do it for me. I did it to connect, to share. I want it to be critiqued. I didn't do this just for myself. I'm not writing this book to read it to myself. I work on it until I'm proud of it and then I share it and I stand on it.

Yes, I want to be seen as the best rapper, but what I have learned is that some people don't see me as the best rapper. Some do. I'm content with that. This is what I feel like separates me from author Malcolm Gladwell. He's one of the greats. I'm cool with Malcolm Gladwell being more celebrated than me as an author.

I'll be content with being another Donald Goines and serving my cult following and writing my books. I would be proud of that. Malcolm Gladwell is like an Eminem, a JAY-Z. They get super detailed and they deserve to be celebrated. I enjoy them. But it takes them years and years to write a book or release a new album. I'm a Donald Goines. The difference between Malcolm Gladwell and me is that I'm going to make more money because I'm going to make so many books for my following and be content on making them good and great. Even if I make $50,000 per book and he makes $5 million, I'm going to make so many fifty grands that I'm going to get past him because I've shielded myself from the criticism that he's got to go through. I'm cool with making twenty books a year, not two. Another author can write two books and they are going to stand the test of time. I know I've still got to sit by my typewriter just like they did. I still wrote a book.

You can enjoy this book or not, but I'm going to make my fifty-second book, my hundred and eighth book. It doesn't matter how long it took me to write it. Every time I write it, I'm going to try to come with something so creative and slick that I feel like I wrote the dopest book ever. I'm doing this because I like to do it and I feel like it's something that I'm good at. Every time I do it, I'm trying to bring something to the world.

I'm like a basketball player. I'm not trying to get crossed over and lose. But if I lose, guess what? I gave it my all. I still had some good shots in there. But you've got to come to play. You can't say, "Damn. We lost. Everybody's cheating." You just can't get distracted. Wake up earlier and get another workout in. Experiment and see how that

feels. "Okay. I wrote one book. They liked that. I'm going to try to write another one kind of like that." But if I look back, I know they had to pay me every time I wrote a book, because I have a contract. So, three years later, I got paid for five books. Now I want a deal for three books at a time.

All this stacks on everything else. That's why being focused and being smart and being wise gives you an advantage. But in the end, *time* is all you got. I realized that a lot of people that I deal with, a lot of young black people growing up in Atlanta, they almost look down on people who are smart or somebody who tries to talk some sense into them. As soon as somebody starts talking to them, they think you're trying to trick them. That's how they think. They're closed-minded. They're content with that because as soon as you start talking to them, they're going to feel uncomfortable. I used to be around them. I was always in their good graces because I don't look down on nobody. I understand it. These are my cousins. These are my neighbors. These are my artists. But I've always seen the value of, "Hey, man. If we're doing business, there's a way we've got to do it. We've got to communicate. People have got to understand what I'm saying."

Time is money. You spend your time wisely, you spend your money wisely. If I dropped my first album, *Trap House*, and it only sold ten thousand CDs, that's my number. I'm not going to get rich off of that, especially if I put it out with somebody else. I'm going to have to start doing this on my own, cut the middle man out. If I'm in a group and we made $4 million and we split $1 million apiece, good. But if they're only giving us fifty grand and I'm the one doing all the singing, at some point, I might need to go solo.

That part of me, I always had that thinking from day one. It's always been a business to me. "How much are you gonna charge me for the beat? How much are you gonna charge me for the studio time?" All this made me approach it so that the business was important, because I always started with my own money.

If I was just an artist who got signed with somebody and got a big advance, then I wouldn't have that responsibility. That's what separates me. I had that responsibility. I had wanted somebody to sign me, but I just didn't have the opportunity. By the time somebody did want to mess with me, I was like, "Okay, I finally got some people wanting to invest with me or partner with me, or even do a joint venture with me. I've got to work that to my advantage." If Def Jam would have given me $1 million, I would have signed with them. I didn't have $100,000, but if I had forty grand, I was willing to risk it. If I had forty grand, I would have put ten grand into making the album and $7,500 into getting a thousand CDs.

But now they'll put me in a position where I'm not getting anything but like twenty-some grand when that happens. Then it has to work. I kept taking those types of gambles. That's when it just made more sense for me to do the rapping, too. So now instead of me having to buy clothes for an artist, all I had to do was just put my clothes in the cleaners. Now I'm thinking like, "Oh. I'm the CEO now." Now you've got to rap good enough to where people like it. So you've got to test the waters. Now go get some free beats. Now pay for some beats, too.

When I first started, my whole thing was, "I want to be a CEO." Especially in Atlanta, I wanted to be the dude who was fly and flashy who has a record label. I want to be able to sign artists. It wasn't like I wanted to be an artist. I want to be Jermaine Dupri. I wanted to have money, go in the club, and keep hustling. That's how it first started with me. I put my time into it. It paid off. I invested my time in me. Now I'm living the return on that investment. Every day, I use my time as wisely as possible.

Refocus and Go Harder

Life. It's a lot to deal with. There are distractions all around us. Every day. It's easy to lose focus. It's okay. That happens. Just make sure to catch yourself, refocus, and go harder.

Even with the weight-loss stuff and getting in shape. So many of my friends said, "I'm going to get in shape like you." My day ones, the ones I went to school with, these are my real friends. They're the ones I really keep in contact with. They're like family. I'm like, "Hey, dog. I'm forty. You're forty-two. You're thirty-eight. You're forty-three. Either you're going to do it or don't. It doesn't matter. Two years from now, your ass is still going to be two years older than you are today."

If you tell me you're going to get in shape and six months from now you're still

fat as hell, don't keep telling me the same thing. Just go ahead and eat that trash and be dead. You're going to be dead at fifty or sixty. We know what happens to people who eat like that. We're at that age now. My momma and daddy died at like sixty, fifty-nine. My mom died last January. My dad died two years before that. But so many friends, nephews, uncles, partners, and friends of mine, they're like, "Okay. Just do what you're going to do." At this point, there's so much information at your fingertips, dog. Whatever people are going to do, they're going to do. If you aren't going to do it to help yourself, you're just going to slowly deteriorate. You need to refocus and go harder.

Whenever I lose focus, I bring myself back to center and go harder. It's like a path. My physical transformation is an outward symbol of an internal transformation. If you say you're going to get in shape, my getting in shape is still going on. You're going to say, "Man, my knees and hips still don't do what I want them to do." Then they're like, "Damn, Gucci. You lost weight. I still can't squat. My hips still ain't open. I'm working out, but why am I still feeling tired?" It's not fun. You can wake up tomorrow with good intentions, but then you're like, "Man. My arm hurts. I've been running but, now my ankle hurts." It's so much shit that goes on, so the question is, are you going to be able to go through this shit? It's like they said in that movie *The Shawshank Redemption*: you're either going to get busy living or get busy dying.

All my books that I read, I read them on the toilet. All the tweets that come out, that's coming from me on the toilet. I'm going to use the bathroom every day, so I'm going to tweet every day. I need something to do while I'm doing it. I find that when I read and work out, I'll feel proud enough to say something, or to deal with something negative that came out. But I don't like being a hypocrite, so I'm not going to say something unless I'm in a positive mind state. So there won't be any tweets coming out unless I feel like I did something that I'm proud of.

As I think about what I'm going to tweet, I know I can't say something that I can't back up, first off. So I already had my chest out when I sent it. The world doesn't know that unless they read about it in this book. I'm always refocusing and going harder.

Just Keep Improving

You've got to constantly improve if you're trying to get to the highest levels of health, wealth, creativity, and personal fulfillment. Whatever it is, you've got to keep improving. You're only as good as your last hit.

There is always someone behind you ready to take your place. If you're not improving, someone else is going to come take your position. On top of that, they're going to do it cheaper than you and better than you. Period. Then you're going to wonder why. You're going to be like, "Damn. I know that guy." But you're going to let somebody come and eat your lunch and shit in your lunch box.

Do you know how you allowed that to happen? You didn't keep your foot on the gas. You stopped improving. Next year, you'll be like, "Damn. Why didn't they pick me? Why didn't I get on that soundtrack?" It's because the other guys are doing something. They're bringing something to the table just as creative, but cheaper.

You can prevent that. You've got to make yourself indispensable. You can't trick somebody into thinking you're indispensable. You have to actually have a skill set. You have to show up and deliver. The numbers have to match what you're doing. You've got to be worth what you say you bring to the table. The only thing you can do is do more and then bring more to the table so you can ask for more. If you do less, you've got less leverage. That's it.

Life is brutal. It's like music—highly competitive. But at least you're aware of it now. Some people think that making a song isn't anything, that it's easy. They're living in la-la land. Look at the *Billboard* charts. There's always new artists popping up you've never heard of. Then there's people like me who have stayed in the game. If you don't improve and refine yourself and your music, someone is always ready to take your place.

People may think it's easy for me to make a song because I've made so many, because I've been making them for a long time. But in the beginning, it wasn't always easy to make a song. It's not always easy to do one now, either. People just look at things like, "Oh. It's the product, a finished product." But a lot of work goes into that product.

It's a lot of work. And with work comes improvement. I went to the studio the other day and I realized that now that I've been making songs for so long, I'm critical of myself. I want to keep pushing myself, and the more prolific I am, the more songs I'm making. Now I'm looking at it like I've got to make better songs. Of course I'm getting better, but at the same time, now it's getting more difficult because you can do the kind of songs you've been doing. It's almost like you're on autopilot but you've got to think bigger than just making the same type of song over and over again.

26

Now I'm like, "How can I make a better song? What can I improve on?" You've got to look at it that way because there's always room for improvement. Or you can go backward. It's going to be one or the other. One of my partners told me the saying, "You're either getting better or you're getting worse."

Some people may be like, "I don't even think about that. I'm cool. I'm going to keep doing what I'm doing." It gives them some kind of joy because they don't have to think about the hard truths of the world. So they're cool with wherever they are in life. This book isn't really for them, for that type of person. This book can help the people I know are going to try to work 365 days a year. I want this book to be for people, for when they take a break they can understand, "Hey, I can't work 365 days a year. It doesn't even make sense. But I'm working smarter now. I'm going to rest today. This week I'm going to take a vacation." Sometimes you'll have planned your vacation and it'll be rained out. That's because you don't control everything. You might have said at the beginning of the year, "This is going to be the window where I'm taking a trip for two weeks and kick back. I'm going to kick back and get in the ocean." But guess what? Those two weeks, a hurricane hits. You're not dictating that. But if you're in the right position and have enough money, guess what? If you've been working hard enough and handling your business, you can just go to the other side of the world if you want to because you can afford it.

When you reach this level, whatever happens, you're in the best situation to deal because you know you can only control what you can control.

The less you need, you more you have: I heard that phrase this year and I think it's a gem. That makes so much sense to me. I understand it. I had bought a high-powered building, this big penthouse building. I used it as an office. I used it as a studio, as a gym. But I didn't stay there. It wasn't my home. So I started thinking about it and it didn't make sense. I was commuting there, but I realized that

I could do all of these things at my house. Now I'm looking around and realizing I have all these things I don't even need. I've got too much stuff.

I didn't need all that stuff. In my mind I thought I did because I thought it would make me more efficient, but actually it was a waste. It took me a minute to see that. I had to actually experience it. I was like, "Damn. This actually has me moving backward because it's got me in two places and it's expensive." I had to improve my situation, so I did.

Do What You Got to Do

Do what you've got to do every day when you get up. Even if it's tough. Even if you're like, "Damn, man. I don't feel like doing this shit, but I'm going to do it." Or you're saying to yourself, "I don't really feel like going to work, but I'm going to do it." Or, "Damn. I could call in sick, but I know I can't. It'd probably be best for me if I did my best to be on time."

Do what you've got to do works in other ways, too. I'm not saying on a street level, per se. Be wise. If there's a bully and there's no way to get around them, then don't do what you've got to do. Don't do something and wind up in jail. I mean that whatever you've got to do to improve your life, step up and do it.

If you say you're tough, that you're bad, that you're resilient, show me resilience. If I keep saying I'm tough and that I've been working on myself across the board, when the challenge comes, I'm going to do what I've got to, whatever that may be. Whatever the attack is and whatever life challenges me with—and I'm not saying a physical attack, but whether it's career-wise, family shit—I know that anything can happen with anybody. The Earth will keep rotating, though. So whatever it is, step to it.

Even if it's, "Hey, man. It's going to take me a year to repair the relationship with my parents, I'm going to start. I'm going to send a text, write a letter." Do that shit. I know that path might be tougher than fighting with somebody. Sometimes you've got to admit you're wrong. On the other hand, you might have to curse somebody out that you took a liking to, but you've grown apart and you see where this is headed. You've got to make a good decision before it comes back to bite you. Do what you got to do, but make the mature choice. Don't be a child about it and let it get on top of you. You've got to be like, "Man. Even though it's my brother or my cousin or my sister, I shouldn't have put that before my daughter. I've got to tell her I'm late because I'm being a good person." Nah. You've got to tell your sister, "I'm not going to be able to make that.

"I've got to do this for my daughter, so I can't even go do this for you. If I mess around with you, I'm going to oversleep tomorrow and not be able to take her where she needs to be. I hate to be like that, but guess what? I'm like that because the backstory is you're not dependable enough. If you were, I probably would try to go harder and do both, but it isn't worth it. So I'm going to go ahead and get my rest, which I need because I've got to do what I've got to do. I'm going to wake up tomorrow and take my daughter where she needs to be. I know I can do that."

You have to know what you need to do and what you don't. When you start cutting out things that cause you stress and problems, you'll see the power that comes from focusing on doing what you've got to do, and then doing it. You have to know when to draw that line, though, so you don't burn yourself out. I talk a lot about pushing yourself in this book. But it is possible to push too hard, to burn out. Know when to rest. Rest is powerful. You've got to recharge the battery.

Leave something on the table from yesterday to do the next day. Don't feel like you've got to do everything today, because you're already chasing your goals. Just stay in front of it. I have goals. I may have a six-week fitness goal, or a three-week fitness goal. It's all dependent on my schedule of what I have to do as far as making money and living. It isn't like I'm dictating that. But I do have a choice. These are the days I'm going out of town. These days I've got to handle this and handle that. These are the days where I don't have to do that. So let me plan for it. Now, when those days come, I'm just handling what I said I'm going to do.

Now I'm efficient. In order to get up in the morning and get it done, I've got to hype myself up. I've got to be my own hype man. I've got to read something that helps. I've got to talk to myself. I have to find something to push me to get going, something that helps me.

Some days, you might wake up and say, "I don't want to do it now." You can keep sitting in the bed and saying you're going to get up. But you haven't gotten up. You're tired. But you better get up, because if you lay back down you may oversleep. So what if you're going to be twenty minutes early. Cool. You've got to get up and handle it. Get it done. Do what you've got to do.

These are tough choices we all have to make. I hope this book brings a little solace to everybody, because that's what we're trying to get to. We hope these little words of wisdom will help you get through your day.

Find Something to Be

I was lucky. I knew I wanted to be a great artist, to be rich, to have financial freedom. Some people don't know what they want to be in life. You have to find something you want to be and then go for it. Trust your gut. Follow your instincts. It could be the type of job you want. It could be the type of attitude you're going to have.

Once you find it, then you have to go after it all the way. I've noticed that how you do one thing is how you're going to do everything. If you say, "I'm going to be responsible," you're either going to overlook some of your responsibilities or you're going to take care of it. That's for anybody. Whatever they've got on the table, they're either 100 percent handling their business or halfway handling their business. You get what you give. Everything is a reflection of that. You might not know what's going on, but the only way I could see it working is if you're going hard.

It's almost like signing an artist. You ain't gotta tell me that your cousin's dope. If he was dope, I would know about him. I'd be trying to find him. I'd be saying, "Does anybody know who this kid is?" If you've gotta tell me about him, or you've got to ask me, "What does he have to do to get noticed?" he's probably got to keep making music. You've got to put in the ten thousand hours.

If you want to be a master violinist, what do you have to do? Practice. Then practice more. Then compete with the other people who practice like you practice. Then let them push you to be even better. Then wake up and do it again. You don't get any solace. I always say to myself, "Damn, I keep feeling like once I hit these goals, I'm going to feel a certain way, but I don't get any solace." I really don't. The only solace you get is what you give to yourself.

It's all in your mind, but nobody realizes that, because everybody's running around being naive because it's hard to deal with reality. It's hard to admit that our choices can help us and hurt us at the same time. Sometimes I put my head down for a month or two and I'll be like, "I'm only doing this." I've got a whole bunch of money, but I'll be like, "Damn, I don't even want a haircut for the next two weeks because I'm not spending any money because I want to reach this goal." It's weird, but if I don't do anything, not getting my hair cut leads to not going outside. Not going outside saves money. If you wanted to, that way of thinking could be to your advantage, but you have to know how to not take it too far.

> **It's hard to admit that our choices can help us and hurt us at the same time.**

Here's another way you could look at it. You could say, "I've got an off day," which you created. "I'm not on the road right now. I'm going to go to the studio. I want to buy some clothes." All these things are costing money. If I go to the studio with the engineer, I've got to pay him. The lights gotta come on. Or I could make the choice and not spend anything. Every day is plus or minus. Were you profitable or not? It's like when somebody has to go to work. Let's use a barber, for instance. How many heads did you cut today? You cannot go to work. You can say, "Damn. I've been going to work every day from ten to six since the beginning of school." But if you miss one of those days, you just missed your peak season. That's on you.

Now next week when all these heads aren't coming in, that was your choice. You might have to cut out going to the club one day so you can be at the shop all day. There's so many choices that everybody's got to deal with to find out if they know what they're doing or not. That barber I was talking about won't be a barber for long if he decides not to cut hair. A barber has to cut hair. Once you find something to be, dedicate yourself to it.

Part II

The Process

Every Day Is a Chance to Get Better

You only have today. You only have this moment. Sometimes I have to remind myself that because it's where opportunities come. Right here, right now. That shit is real. It's a daily thing. Every day I only have this moment. The past is gone and the future hasn't come. Today is a blessing. Wake up, realize that today is an opportunity to get better.

When you decide to change your life, you start to visualize everything. You find a vision for your future self. Your fit body. Your new car. That fancy house. But you have to be realistic and take things one day at a time.

I talked to Kevin Gates at the top of the year. We hadn't talked in a minute and were just checking in, wishing each other well. He told me, "You know I always respected you and Jeezy since back in the day for creating the trap shit." It had me going back. I told him, "I respect any-body who makes something out of what they got."

Then we started talking about signing artists. I said, "If I don't sign any artists and I don't make any money off of them, that's just one revenue stream that I don't make. If I don't do shows and I retire, I'm not going to be able to live off what I used to do, unless my catalog's making money. But if I signed that off to somebody, then I won't make anything off that, either. I'd have to live with that con-sequence. Or I've got to keep working to leverage getting it back."

I can respect a platinum artist whose music came out before me, but he's in a different situation than me. Whatever his fate is, it's what he did. I was telling Gates, "Whoever the next artist is, I want the intel on him. I want to be able to compete with signing him now because I still have to go to work today."

Even when people praise me, I appreciate that. But I can't live off that. You've got to find yourself something where you can maintain or increase what you've got going, or it's going to decrease. If you take things one day at a time, you're less likely to do something foolish, to do too much or not enough. You're not looking for that quick money grab, that shortcut. It's the grind, the process that's important.

Look at an artist that came out in the last ten years, twelve years. I've seen all the rap and R&B artists. Even if they were dope as hell and creative, you see how they're living now. A lot of it is their fault. They could have parlayed their name and livelihood into having a better situation. One that lasts. They didn't have to end where they started, which is with nothing. If I had those opportunities or you had them, we could have made the most out of them. I'm sure if they look back, they'd probably say, "Damn. I wish I had done some things differently. I would've been in a better position. If I would have signed that artist instead of shunning them, if I would have befriended these people, maybe I would have some people that would have paid some shit forward. Now I'm like, 'Damn. I hope I have something to fall back on. I wish I was trying to sign these artists.'" But you can't skip any steps. You've got to do the groundwork. And the groundwork happens day by day.

It's the same thing with being rich. If I'm a new artist and you give me $1 million and I spend $200,000 or $300,000 of it, even if I make another $1 million in the next couple of years, if I'm bad and overspend, in two or three years, that's gone. It's a fast burn. But it doesn't have to go that way.

You've got to have a plan and the plan has got to be flexible. That's why I said I had to learn to take it day by day, because I get so rigid and locked into a plan sometimes. I might be like, "Okay. This is 2020. This is what I'm going to do this year." I would fuck around and forget to have any fun for the first four months of the year. That's because my head was down trying to lay down what I said I was going to do. My plans used to put me in a rigid box. And it's like, "Damn. You still don't get the time back." If you're thirty-five, now you're thirty-seven and it's like, "Damn. I missed a lot of shit those last two, three years." Know where you're going but focus on what you can do today.

You've got to find a balance. Every day I've got to keep myself rooted and balanced. I've got to remember, "Hey. Life is more than just accumulating a bunch of money. What are you going to do with it? You still have to live." Life is a journey. It's not, "Hey. I got here and I can reward myself. Ha. I'm good." Nah. You've got to plan to live and to leave a legacy, too. When you start thinking like that, all your days count. Even if you just say, "I'm going to have some rest today and get some sleep." Or if you say, "I think I might need to have a vacation and rejuvenate my mind." Even if you're thinking about death. You'll start planning for that if you're thinking for the long run.

Look Up, Look Down, Then Look Around

You've got to look at the big picture. There's more than one way to skin a cat. There's more than one option. There are many paths forward, and the one you think is it might not be the right path. Stop, pause, and look at your life from every angle. You don't have to drop one album every year. If you've got to drop ten albums a year to make the same amount of money as somebody that made one album, do it.

Don't let anybody tell you, "This is how it's got to go." If you can't make it in the NFL, go to another league. Go to the Canadian league. Start coaching. Own the team. Be the offensive coordinator. Be the running-back coach. Start with coaching high school. Go overseas and play. Don't let anything define you. Look up, look around, and find a way.

Basically, there's no excuse. Figure it out. Go to school online. Take out a loan. Get a part-time job. It's okay if it's going to take you nine years to graduate. Do it. What's stopping you? What are you going to do instead? Hang on the corner? Once you learn how to change the narrative, it's easier to look all around you for the real picture.

Everybody knows that person from where they grew up that is still in the same hood doing the same thing. That shit's sad, man. I've got a couple friends I went to elementary school with that I still keep up with, that I still keep around. I can monitor my progress by looking at them. We're the same age and we went through the same things. I can look at them and be like, "I need to watch what I'm doing." I can also pick up game from them. "Damn, he's dedicated. Damn, he's super responsible. Damn. I like how my dog's maturing and growing." It's the same things that they can say about me. I try to keep them in my life, but at the same time, it gives you a sense of what you're doing right and what they're not doing right.

But remember, everybody isn't at the same place. Period. Some of us are singers. Some of us are married. Some of us are chasing girls. Some are serving time. Everybody's got different shit going on. Look around you.

People forget they can learn from anything and everyone. Lessons abound. When somebody makes a mistake, you can learn from that. You can't be looking at it like, "I can't pay attention to that dude. He makes mistakes." You can look at someone and see the right moves to make and the wrong moves to make.

Look at me. I had a choice. I wanted to be a comeback story, a redemption story. It doesn't always have to end negatively. It can end well. But it isn't going to happen overnight. People look at me and think my transformation happened easily. It didn't. It took years and years of dedication. *Years*. I took the principles I'm telling you about now and tried to put them in motion every day. Sometimes I did. Sometimes I didn't. But I dedicated myself to doing these principles as often as possible. Yes. It took years and it will take years. It will never stop. This is not a diet. This is a lifestyle.

You might have to work the job you don't like until you get something else. They might say, "Just to get out of jail, you might have to work at McDonald's." You know good and well that you're not going to work at McDonald's forever. But can you work at McDonald's for three months, work at a warehouse for three months to get outta jail so now you can really start your business that you have a game plan for? If you aren't willing to do that, you're not willing to do anything. McDonald's or the warehouse is a mild sacrifice when you think about it. You've got to break yourself down to build yourself up.

You have to say, "Okay. I'm going to humble myself to do what I've got to do." That's all it is. Whatever the burden or challenge is, it's not going to move out of your way. Wishing isn't going to help. The only way to do it is slowly and methodically, and by preparing your mind to do it. That's how you've got to handle it if you're not privileged and you don't have the resources to just do what you want to do. The reason I wanted to do this book is to touch the people that's going through something. It's not going to be easy. But start now.

Look up, look down, look around. You have to take inventory. What is working for you? What isn't? Who is good for you? What is good for you? You have to look at everything in every direction, and in every way. It's not going to take a minute. It's going to take years. It's going to take ten thousand hours if you're trying to master it. You're going to have so much to say and do during the journey if you're going to be successful. But start.

Embrace Every Challenge

I'm proud of me. Look at what I'm doing and what I used to do. I'm feeling good about myself because I overcame all of this shit. There were always people doubting me. Now, you're either with me, or you're against me. I got to where I'm at because of challenges. Challenges to my success as an artist, my health, my relationships. Every obstacle that I encountered, I embraced. Every setback, and I've had my share, was an opportunity to embrace failure, learn, and turn it into a challenge.

I made an album in 2019 called *Delusions of Grandeur*. I named it that because I had gotten into good physical shape. I was really confident at the time. I didn't want to take my hand off the wheel, get too cocky, and revert to things I used to do. Instead of acting like I don't have it under control, I'm going to put out into the world that I'm having delusions of grandeur right now. I knew that this shit could crash.

That was my way of crashing without crashing. That's how weird I had to talk to myself. That's what helps me. Instead of trying to sneak it there, I put it out in public.

When I rap, I make so much music, three, four, five albums a year. I'm rapping about what's going on with me in that time of my life. So I was like, "Don't try to sneak it in and say, 'Hey, man. This is what I'm doing.'" Even if the fans wouldn't have liked it, I had to do it.

Sometimes it's not going to sell because some of this stuff is just too personal. It's personal to me. But even if it's just personal, that I'm doing good and I'm balling because that's what's going on with me, you might not want to hear that. You might want to hear J. Cole or Kendrick Lamar or 2Pac, and that's going to make them sell more albums. I'm cool with selling whatever I sell, so I'm processing that, being grateful for what I did and then approaching something totally new.

That is the craziest thing I told all my artists, and it's something I don't know that everyone understands. If you've got even one fan, that's the beginning and you need that. Starting is the biggest challenge of all. You're on your way. You're good. You're done. You should never be depressed. Now it's on you. Are you going to work? Period. Embrace that challenge.

If I like an artist and they drop a tape right now, and they have a small following, it's just simple math, man. If you drop another good project, man, you're going to have those same followers, plus more. You can only lose them by doing things that are going to put you in the negative. So do the things to stay in front of that, man. You're good. So this is how you judge yourself. You say, "Hey man, I'm going to do this for a year and see what happens."

But if a year later you're saying, "I put out two projects. One did thirty thousand and the next one did twenty. It ain't worth it. I'm going to do something else." Or you say, "I put out one that did twenty, and the next one did twenty, I'm going to try it another year." Now you've got something to look at, to judge yourself on. That's where I'm at. Some people are like, "Ah, man. They didn't like that." I don't give a damn if I sold five thousand, if I sold five million—I'm still pushing another album.

Look at my song "Proud of You," off my *Delusions of Grandeur* album. I got a good response. I had been working hard on myself. It was almost like my victory lap. I was in a good space all around. So it was like, "Don't run from that." Be happy that you're doing well. When you put on an outfit, sometimes you want to say, "Damn. I'm fresh as hell." You want to tell your wife, "Baby, we look good tonight. Let's go out. Let's go dance." I'm not saying it to be cocky or arrogant.

Now if I go and tip my nose up like I feel like I'm doper than him, it's different. If I say, "Look at where I'm at and where I came from. I'm feeling good about myself. I'm proud of myself. I'm telling you why."

The real question is, how could you not be happy for that person? They embraced their challenge. How could anyone not be happy for Demi Lovato coming back from an overdose in 2018 to perform at the Grammys in 2020? How could that not touch you? That can't make you mad, can it?

I wanted to lean on that type of thing. I wanted to go do a video and show people. It was almost like a mixtape. I recorded the songs and did the photo shoots all in one day. Every song was me. I put it out like an album. It's almost like I'm doing mixtapes and saying they were albums. That's how I treated all of my projects in 2019.

It was almost like I'm just having fun, like author Donald Goines. I made my hundredth album. Then I made my hundred and first one, and my hundred and second one because I know if I dropped an album in May, it would have been my hundred and third. If I make three albums in 2020 like I did in 2019, I'll be up to 105 albums, which means I'll have been putting out seven albums a year for fifteen years. That's a stellar career, to me. Then I look back and add up my money and say, "I'm proud of what I've become. I didn't get played. I am a businessman, even if I'm only managing my damn self. I'm managing myself well."

When I look back at my life, I see someone who has had success and failure. When I look back at my life, I see someone who embraced every challenge.

Work in Silence

That's super, super important. It's also super relevant right now. Silence is a vote of confidence in yourself. You need to do the work because it needs to be done, not because you want to be seen doing it. Let the work speak for itself. When the time is right, people will notice and be like, "Man. I didn't know he was doing that."

You don't always need to have your mouth running. Once you tell somebody what you've done, I feel like you lose all credibility because it's almost like you're telling people to pat you on the back. It's vain. I look at it almost like charity. If you're giving from the heart, you don't say anything. If you say something to somebody about what you did, then you gave for a return. Then some people give to have other people under their thumb. Wise people give and never say things. Wise people give without expecting the return. They know the return is coming in time.

I always operate with the truth. Look, I'm not saying that all these things are going to make your life perfect. I don't want people to read this book and think that I don't ever mess up. I mess up all the time, but I'm aware of it and I never let it get me down. If I do something that's not part of my priorities, I'll be like, "Damn. Okay. I just spent a whole week being off task." I then get back to the task in silence.

Life's still going to go on. Everybody else just had the same week. But me, I'm going back to reality. I understand that, so let me get back on task. Let me try and stay on task for two or three days. That'll compensate for the mistakes I just made, and once I get to the point where I want to be, I'll deal with that when I get there. But it's not just about putting one foot in front of each other as you march ahead. Demand more out of yourself. Demand that you'll do it right. Do it in silence.

Be Resilient

I've gone through so many things, from a difficult childhood, to going to jail, to trying to come up as a rapper. What has kept me resilient through my life? Self-talk and en-couraging myself are what made me shake it off and be prolific instead of being down on myself and being in the dumps. Self-talk helps keep me productive and in a hyped stage. It got me out of the hole and hyped me up, like a fighter. When I'm up against the ropes, I tell myself, "I'm going to get through this. I know what they're saying, but I'm going to show everybody and show myself that this isn't going to be the end of me." By putting it out there and saying that, you're going to start doing things every day to do that.

It takes so much discipline to be resilient. Being persistent and being resilient, it's about doing the shit once you fall down, once the haters are laughing at your mistakes. Resilience is about bending instead of breaking. You need to keep your focus and follow your passion, even when nobody's around.

What are you going to do when nobody's around? It was comfortable for me to go into the studio all the time with my artists and to smoke weed. It was productive as far as putting out music. But it wasn't hard to do. It was staying in my comfort zone. It's hard to wake up every day and do a job efficiently and then on top of this, I'm going to add a hobby. On top of this, I'm going to have another job. On top of this, I'm going to have a long end game of doing something else. On top of this, I'm going to dedicate time to volunteering with the intention of building something with it.

You keep doing that day in and day out, you're going to get tired when people aren't looking. But it's even harder when you're in the public eye, because if you tell me something, everyone can check on

it. If you say, "Hey. I'm here and I'm three hundred pounds. I'm going to start losing weight. This is me in the gym. Boom." If I see you lose the weight, I'm proud of you. But when I see you put the weight back on, I can see that you got distracted. So, you can't be telling me, "Hey, man. Don't lose focus," because I can see you're drunk as hell. You're missing two or three shows and that's in the public, just like other stuff that you put in the public and tried to get me to follow you on. Be resilient through your words and action.

Have faith that the hardship will pass. Know that whatever happens does not forever define you. Resilience is knowing that another outcome is on the other side. Resilience is weathering the storm.

Part III

Account-ability 101

Everybody Must Be Held Accountable

It is hard to look in the mirror and see the truth. It's hard to judge yourself. People create their own narrative of who they are, and it's not always rooted in reality. It's hard to be brutal on yourself. Every day, I critique what I ate. In my self-talk, I'm like, "Damn, man. I could have done better. Damn, I was kind of undisciplined in the things I said. I could have watched what I said, the tone I used. I could have done better in that meeting, been more open. I was aggressive for no reason." It's easy to just brush it off when you know you weren't operating at a high level. It's a defense mechanism. But I'm like, "Damn, I need to do better. With this meeting tomorrow, I'm going to do better." Then tomorrow I ask myself, "Did I do better?" All these things, it's easy to not deal with them. You can go through the whole day without having that conversation with yourself. I reflect. I keep myself in check. I hold myself accountable.

I didn't start doing that until I was thirty-three, the last time I was locked up. I took a real tough look at myself and a real tough look at my life. I had hit my bottom. Things had gotten totally out of my control. I was either going to wind up dead or in prison. Before, I knew my crimes would result in a worst-case scenario of six months' time. Now it would be like I could be gone for fifteen years, twenty, or life. That was traumatic to me. My career would be gone. My life would be gone.

I came to peace with the realities of my situation. I decided I was going to do everything in my power to do better with the things in my control. And what is the one thing you can control? Yourself. I needed to be in a place to handle my life. Mentally, physically. I was in survival mode. Then it went from survival mode to, "Man, I can use this for more. I can use this to be productive. Damn. If I can just be in better shape, I can do even more in twenty-four hours than I used to do." I knew I could take on even more responsibilities. I knew I could achieve sustained greatness. As you start practicing it and keep on doing it, you start being more and more efficient. You're getting sharper.

This is a thing I used to separate myself from my peers. As of 2020, I've been rapping for fifteen years. A lot of people that were hot back in 2005, when I first came out with *Trap House*, are not out today. They may have made hit records ten years ago but they can't leverage those wins. Even though they went platinum, they don't have any money now. They fell off. Their marriage is slipping. Their finances are slipping. They probably had stuff that went on with their record label. They've got infighting and can't put stuff out. They don't have the same team and everything went roller coaster down. My longevity isn't an accident, it is by design.

That's why I always try to look at myself. Reflect, keep myself in check, hold myself accountable. As I move forward, I can trace whatever happens back to pivotal times in my life. It's easy for me to tell when I was making good decisions and when I was making bad decisions. You can ask me, "When did you start thinking like that?" I'm like, "This is when it was going good. This is when it was going bad." It's like a graph. This is when I had my best year. This is when I had my worst. When I was in my best times, what was I doing? What was I doing then that could help me now? Sometimes the opportunity isn't going to be there anymore. It's squandered. It's gone.

I got a homeboy that's twenty-six and I got another friend who's thirty-one. One of them is a trainer and the other one is a coach. I was like, "Ya'll are so smart. You've been working on your body, your mind. You went to college. You have these social skills that a lot of people don't have because they don't value them." But as far as talking to somebody and articulating those values, they never did that. They never valued that. Even when I was in the streets, it was something that I knew, like, "Hey, man. I can do this a little bit better than the next person can," or I would step to a person and talk to them. That opened up business. There are so many things that you can practice on that other people don't have. Now a person sees that they're forty years old and their opportunities are squandered. They've burned so many bridges when they were young. When they had their chance, they didn't treat people right. They didn't know how to talk to them because they just didn't have the skills.

For a lot of these people who were hot fifteen years ago, it doesn't matter now—all of those platinum songs. They might have signed their publishing away. They might not get booked now. They might have child support. Their money is gone.

I feel like the only way you can succeed and get where you want to be, is that *you can't quit*. I'm not just saying that with rapping. You could be playing basketball, be on the radio, journalism, whatever. The things that I'm saying apply to anything you're trying to do. That's why I said, "Don't get distracted." If you start at the mail room and you work your way up to VP and now you're the president, you should demand shares. You can own the company or be a partner in it. Or you can go to another company where you can make that happen. Or you can start your own company. There's always another level. There's always another step. You don't have to deteriorate. You can always learn more. You can always gain new skills.

I didn't know that when I was going in and out of jail all the time. I didn't know what accountability was about.

I learned it by default. I was facing a situation where I hit rock bottom. I was like, "If I do get these ten years, I want to be in the best possible shape mentally, physically." I wanted to be able to deal with it. As you start dealing with that, your reality turns into, "Hey, man. That's not on the table anymore, to be acting foolishly and making bad decisions." Now I'm reading books, working out, thinking differently. I'm in a whole different mindset now. Now I can take in more knowledge. So instead of me cutting off and being like, "Okay. I weathered that storm. I'm good," what if I actually say, "I do appreciate this, this hand I've been dealt. It is a blessing. It is an opportunity." If I'm really appreciative and don't take it for granted, I'm going to parlay that into an opportunity. That's my way of showing appreciation: by being real, by being accountable. My accountability is my gift to myself.

Self-Discipline Brings Riches

That's a rule I live by. You have to stay self-disciplined. You need to stay goal-oriented. You have to hold yourself accountable. These are the essentials I apply to my own life, my own routine. Those principles got me where I am today. One thing I value right now is a routine. That's something that's helpful and positive. It keeps me on track. But to hold yourself to a routine, you've got to stay disciplined. Arrange your day and your time to benefit where you're trying to go, or whatever goals you've got. Have a goal. I make it a point to wake up early, to think, to plan, to work out, to spend time with my family, to record, to get ready for my trips, to perform. That's a part of my routine, which helps me stay on my goals.

You've got to have short-term and long-term goals. You've got to reevaluate your goals periodically to make sure that the goal is worth obtaining and that it's not a waste of time. Find something to be excited about every day. Have some kind of long-view game. Be detached from the outcome. Pray and have faith that whatever you're doing, some kind of way some help is going to come. Plan for a surprise. Detach from the outcome. Know what you've got and know that help is coming.

I developed goals in my recording career, both short-term and long-term. I wanted to stay in the game and keep putting out product. I knew it wouldn't be easy, but I was driven to be successful, to be rich. Musically I'd compare myself to an E-40 or a Tech N9ne. That's where it comes to my mind because they're still doing it and they didn't retire. They keep going. They keep *going*. They are disciplined. They've been at it over thirty years. A long time in this business. The amount of music that's put out, and the fact that they keep going and they're still creative. They still have fan bases. Even if it's a thousand fans, they're going to keep cultivating those same fans.

With my music, it was never about being a rapper or waking up making music. It was always, "How can I be creative enough to be productive enough to make a living off of rap? How can I turn my 2005 tax returns into a big one?" By 2007, it was, "How can I employ more people? How can I sign better artists?" The albums were just a tool to get me where I'm trying to get to, which is financial freedom. That's how I always approached rapping. It was different for me. I didn't start rapping at eighteen and immediately was dope. It wasn't a childhood passion of mine, something I dreamt about as a kid. Even though people celebrate me like that, that's not who I am.

What makes me motivated every day is handling my business, staying in front of stuff. I don't want to lose. I don't want to lose money, my health, my wife, my family. I have to be disciplined to keep all that I've worked for, and to keep building on it. That's what I'm doing that I think most rappers aren't doing, most people aren't doing. You can take basketball and translate that to business, that attitude, that approach. It

The minute you let go of your discipline is the moment you give up on yourself.

works regardless of what you do for a living. Self-discipline is the key to unlocking everything you're trying to do. You want to know how important it is? The minute you let go of your discipline is the moment you give up on yourself.

I want to show people, "Look at how my life has changed. This is what I do daily. This is my mentality." That's why there are so many pictures in here. This is what I did for the last two years. This is what I was thinking. Stay focused. Stay disciplined. Like I say, self-discipline brings riches.

Self-Awareness Is a Valuable Weapon

Once you start purposefully planting the seeds of greatness in your life, they're going to start manifesting in all kinds of ways. You have to be aware of what you're doing, the steps you're taking to improving your life. But nobody knows how the seed is going to sprout. I don't even know how my things will sprout. But I know if you put in the work, you're going to get results. But to give the seed the environment it needs to grow, you need to be self-aware.

No matter what your goals are, if you put a plan into action and see it through, you're going to reach those goals. Then you might need more goals. The goals never stop. But I guarantee you that you won't get anything if you don't do anything.

I can't tell everybody, "Hey, man. Don't drink liquor. Don't smoke. Don't do drugs." I can't say that, because everybody who does drugs doesn't always end up having to go to rehab or end up being a junkie. But I've never heard nobody say they drank their way to good health, or that they smoked their way to good health. Everybody's not going to be messed up, but you know that the people that don't do it tend to have a healthier life. I'm not saying that they won't get hit by a car. But if they're more aware because they don't drink, they'll be less likely to crash.

It's small things like that that accumulate over time. You might be the one who doesn't fall asleep behind the wheel because you aren't high. You might be the one who saves someone's life because you say, "Hey. I'm going to drive for you, homie." Or you say, "I know that drinking and smoking aren't against the law, but we might need to take an Uber. Because you drove, I got it." You might just be the one to make that mature decision. That might be the "aha" moment because it saved everybody's life, but people don't think like that.

These decisions you make, they build over time. That goes for the good and the bad. If you start making one bad decision, then you make another one. Then they compound. It's like a numbers game.

But it's not a game. It's life. Look at a garden, for instance. You mean to tell me there are four seasons and if I plant this season and tend to my garden, there's going to be a time when plants sprout and then I can actually harvest them and take them to the market? You mean to tell me I can do that same thing again next year? Yes. Everybody can. That's a growth mindset. That's playing the long game, staying self-aware, again and again. That's the trick of life. It's not a game. Once you are aware of that, you will be like the garden and you'll start growing.

This is with everything. If you don't tend to your garden, it's going to decay and turn fallow. That also applies to your mind, your body, your spirit, your marriage, your business, your body, your brain, your brand. It's like a bank account. If you keep taking stuff out and don't put anything in, what's going to happen? You may not lose everything right away. Your people will be like, "Damn. They used to have so much money and they went broke." Then they may do an interview, and the interviewer may be in awe. They may ask, "Did you hear what happened with the artist that fell off?" I look at it differently. This is what I feel like separates me and makes me say I'm cut from a different cloth. I look at as simply, like, "Okay. How old was that person when they lost everything? How much money did they have? What did they buy? Okay, they were married at that time? Okay, they were gambling at the time?" That's self-awareness at work.

What if somebody said, "Well, Gucci sent me a gift the other day. Even though we've got a business together, that was a surprise. That was appreciated and it was real because he put a note in there. It said, 'Hey. I can't make it to the party, but I sent you this gift.' That was a surprise to me. I appreciated that." That doesn't happen a lot, somebody just genuinely sending you something, just a thanks, without any expectation of anything in return. There's almost always something attached to it.

On the other side of it, people do things that are disrespectful. We all know it. It's happened to all of us a bunch of times. Like with young artists that are high. They call you with this or that issue and you're like, "Damn. I'm grown. Me and my grown partners, we don't handle each other like this." But young folks handle stuff like that because, guess what? They're high. They're immature. They're irresponsible. Knowing that, I grade people on a curve. A lot of people don't understand that approach. I apply my self-awareness to the realities of other people's situations. I understand when people say they're ready to throw in the towel, when they feel like they're up to their limit.

It's because we give a lot of ourselves to people who aren't putting as much thought into life as we are. We are responsible, but not everyone we deal with is. We've got to be the big brother. That will help bring you off the ledge. You've got to stop acting like you're surprised, that you're surprised somebody did something they were supposed to do. After the thirteenth time you told me that type of thing, do you want me to be a shoulder to cry on? What are we doing? At some point, it is what it is and you adjust accordingly so you don't get caught slipping or in a bad situation.

When I tell my wife, "Babe, I can't *believe* this just happened." She's like, "Okay. Well, believe it, because it's here." She's right. Now I've got to fix my mind, my mentality. Once I'm straight, then I'm like, "There's nothing we can do about this but call a lawyer because yes, this is unfair. This is unjust. It's vindictive." I'm just saying that to anything that happens to me. It's the only way I respond, because I know one thing: I've worked so hard that I'm not doing anything illegal. I haven't broken any laws. I've got plenty of money, and everything I have, I feel like I've earned it. I try not to go anywhere unless I've paid to go there. I feel like I have every right to be protected. So if anything happens to me, it's going to the lawyer.

Stay aware of yourself and others. Be able to look at yourself objectively. Know where your head is at. Awareness is a valuable weapon.

Part IV

Your People

Choose Your Friends Carefully

Even when I was a kid, I started seeing that I was different. I had big dreams and many of the people around me didn't. Watch who you choose as friends. Your circle can be your biggest asset or your biggest liability. Friends are there to give advice. But there is good advice, and there is bad advice. Don't take advice from the wrong people.

Some of my friends that dropped out of school in the eighth or ninth grade, they might have had success. But it was limited. I started seeing that same type of person in a lot of the artists I was signing and a lot of people I was working with. I was like, "Damn. Some people don't learn and they don't care." They're cool with that because they live the type of life where they only have to interact with other people like that. I could take you to Atlanta and you wouldn't even understand what the people there are saying. It's almost like they're talking a different language. But the crazy thing is, it's not proper English. It's not how you're supposed to talk. I realized these are not the people I wanted to follow, to seek advice from. We didn't have the same goals, the same dreams, the same objectives. I was thinking worldwide. They were thinking local.

Everybody is not going to understand you. That's straight-up. It's the truth. But it was no big deal to be like that in East Atlanta, in Alabama. But to me, I'm like, "Damn. Nobody seems to care. I do." Some of my friends, they've lived a different life. They don't even know how blessed they are, that they got to play sports overseas. They got that experience, that culture. I was like, "You just don't know. I'm just now getting my passport." This is different for me. When I'm in another country, I definitely feel like a tourist, but at the same time, I'm glad I got to the point where I can embrace somebody with different experiences. Some people, they're scared of that. They're closed-minded.

I had my first international tour when I still had my ankle monitor, but they allowed me to go. It was 2017, right before I got off of house arrest. Right before I got off the ankle monitor, my probation officer was like, "You're doing well. I'm going to let you go on the tour." I got booked for like ten shows. I went to Paris. I went to Germany. I went to Denmark, Belgium. But I was just so happy that I could go get the money. It was good to be able to go somewhere and to travel. I was really glad that I could be like, "I can add this to my repertoire." I was parlaying opportunities. That was the biggest thing. Now I can do shows in America and I can go over there. I'm glad my probation officer wasn't being a dick and didn't say I couldn't go.

After I came back, I had two years left on probation. But I was doing so well that they let me off probation two years early. Now, I could go wherever I wanted. He told me that he'd seen the way I'd been approaching everything. Getting off of probation when I got

out, that kind of helped me too, because he was telling me that he was watching me, everything I did, everything I posted. I was putting out an image of only things that were positive.

If somebody was around that was a felon, he said he would violate me. So now I couldn't be around felons for a year. Now that they were making me go through all of these things, I had to keep myself occupied because I didn't want to violate my parole and have to go back to jail. Now when I got out of jail, I knew I had to do something for a year straight and I had to post it on social media because I didn't want my probation officer to think I was on some bullshit.

It worked out in my favor and I told my wife, "I'm not even going to tell people I'm off probation. I'm just going to keep on acting like I was because it was like a defense." People were like, "I know he's on probation and he's got that thing on his ankle. I don't want to see him get messed up. I'm not going to be around him." I just rolled that out. That whole routine I had, I just never stopped.

I didn't always keep the right company. So I started to choose my friends more carefully. I didn't want the wrong people getting in my ear, in my mind. I wanted the people who were giving me advice to be the right ones.

Avoid Lazy and Miserable People

That's one of the key things you can tell yourself every day. Avoid lazy and miserable people. When you start living by this principle, you're looking in the mirror and telling yourself, "Hey man, I expect a lot out of you." You're demanding the best out of yourself. You are your best asset. And when you get rid of people around you who might disrupt that, you stop being naive. You become more aware. A lazy and miserable mindset leads to a lazy and miserable life. So avoid lazy and miserable people.

Look at whatever you're procrastinating on. Work. Exercise. Taxes. Cleaning. Studying. Reading. You can be like, "I know I need to do this but I'm going to act like I don't." Or, "Damn it. I know my health is failing me but fuck it, I'm going to still keep eating unhealthily." That's lazy thinking.

Let's say one day you woke up and wrote it down. And lived by that mantra. "I'm going to avoid lazy, miserable people every day." Now you're aware of it. So even if it's members of your family, you're going to avoid them. That's a job in itself. Once you can put that out there and you're thinking like that, you're on the right path.

Living by that guideline changed my life. I didn't realize it, but I used to have a lot of people like that in my life. They were miserable and they didn't always have my best interests in mind. When I noticed that, and I noticed that we had different goals, I also noticed that they were distracting me and sidetracking me. I had been blind to that. So I made a change. I made my circle right and have done my best to do it that way from now on.

And I'll never go back. It orients me in the right direction every morning. It puts me in a different bracket. Not a different tax bracket—a different social bracket, a different mental bracket. You're only as good as the company you keep. You're only going to associate with people who are driven, who are trying to get the most out of their twenty-four hours. You're not going to hang around the slacker or the oversleeper. You're going to hang around the early bird, the overachiever.

The change and the success you experience, it's not going to be by luck. It's going to be by choice.

You choose to be naive about what you want to be naive about. It's almost as if you were being a parent. Have you ever been in the supermarket or the airport and seen an unruly, spoiled child? The kid is just acting entitled. You witness that and you're like, "Damn." You know immediately they ain't acting right. But it'd be different if it was your child, or your nephew or your little brother. It would be a whole different dynamic. You might not be as aware, because it's family. It's not a big deal, but it's a big deal to the bystander, because some behaviors are clearly out of line. But we choose to be naive about what we want to be naive about.

Why are we like that? Because we do things that are comfortable. I shouldn't eat the cheeseburger, the ice cream. But eating the cheeseburger and the ice cream makes me feel better. It makes me comfortable, so I'm going to make that choice. I'm gonna eat the cheeseburger and the ice cream. That was the old me. Cheeseburgers, ice cream . . . codeine. Everybody has to deal with temptation. How do I get back in better health? I make a better choice. I decide to drink water, drink a smoothie or something like that. I'll just make a better choice. But, ultimately, the choice is mine. You choose to be naive. You choose to be lazy.

Some people say, "Man, there isn't enough time in the day." They're always tired. Other people, they get everything done and they go to sleep tired. Which one are you going to be?

Haters Are Going to Say You Were Cloned

People look at the positive change with my life, my mind, and my body and they say, "I can't do what he's doing, so what can I do to discredit it?" They say those types of things because it's too hard to say, "I can't do it."

You feel that way because it's hard and you don't want to say or to admit to yourself that you don't want to put in the effort to make the changes necessary to change your life. Sure, everybody wants to be healthy. Everybody wants to look their best. Everybody knows there's a couple of things you've got to refrain from and a couple of things you got to do that aren't going to be enjoyable. It's straight like that. Suffering is part of it.

So if they don't want to deal with that, if they don't want to hold themselves accountable, they've got to discredit someone who has done it. That's the mindset of people who don't want to take it upon themselves to create the change they want to see. They look at others who have succeeded and try to take that away from them. When I got out of jail in 2016 I was a new man. The public couldn't believe their eyes. They said I was cloned. A lot of people thought Gucci wasn't going to hold course. They were wrong.

Here's what I live by. Don't overeat. Get good amounts of rest. Stay in an even temperament. Have a good routine. Do everything you've got to do to earn money. Know that working on your mind or working on your body is not a hobby or a pastime. It's as important as anything you'll ever do. Once you get into that zone, these things are going to put you in a community of people that give you depth. You can't do these things alone, especially if you're trying to do them properly. These things are going to have you going to different levels that require different people to come into your circle.

If you are already doing what you're supposed to do, you're going to be a benefit to the people in your circle. They're also going to be a benefit to you. Now you get more out of yourself than just your abilities. The foundation is built. It's natural. But you can also be a part of some toxic things and your stuff could be shifting to negativity. You could be going the other way. I've been on both sides. The majority of people I've seen, the people that I hang around, the people in my family, the people in America, the people worldwide—they're not taking that tough challenge. So they aren't reaping the benefits or the rewards of a good life, a healthier life. They have the potential. We all have the potential, but many of us aren't making the right choices.

Why don't we make the right choices? Because it is not easy. It doesn't always come natural. It is hard work. It took me years to think about it like, "Damn, if I feel the way that I'm feeling, why wouldn't everybody start taking the steps that I'm taking?" Somebody told me it's because a lot of people don't even know that they feel bad. They think the way they feel is normal. It might be their normal, but it doesn't have to be. I say, "I feel good." They say they don't know what feeling good is. The aches and pains and bumps and bruises, they're definitely feeling them. But it's just a part of their normal life, a daily thing.

> They said I was cloned. A lot of people thought Gucci wasn't going to hold course. They were wrong.

That's how life is for them. They run through life like that. They end up passing away and never get to experience a healthy life, a life without aches and pains. Those type of people, they're going to say you were cloned because they don't want to put that work in to get themselves right.

Women Are Brilliant

Pay attention to women. They are brilliant. Women have changed my life, again and again. Women give great advice. A lot of men think they know everything and are old-fashioned in their relationships and don't listen to their woman. I've never been like that, but I know so many of my friends growing up felt like they were smarter than their baby mommas. My friends just disregarded them and almost everything they said. That's naive thinking. I would look at my friends like, "Nah. You're stupid. She's smart. You should shut the fuck up and listen to her. She's telling you to stay home. Don't go out and get in trouble, because there's a high percentage you are not coming back. She sees it. She's got eyes."

Listen closely to whoever the woman in your life is. She's a genius. She's watching you. You're important to her. If you've got a woman that feels like you're important to her, she has to talk to you and communicate with you. Nine times out of ten, it is not to your detriment. It is to your benefit.

If she's telling you something to your detriment, then you know you're already in a bad position and you've got the blind leading the blind. That's just the truth. It can be that she says something and you're not listening, or she's telling you the wrong thing and you're both going to crash. That's already a problem.

You can't put a lion and a tiger together and think they aren't going to fight. They're going to fight. It is what it is. Just like the lion and tiger, you can't put two aggressive people together. If they have a shared issue or a hatred toward each other, and you can't put them with a bunch of people and you throw them in the room and expect everything to be good, for everyone to be calm, what do you think is going to happen, more than likely? A fight is going to happen. But if you put two cool, calm people together that communicate well, they might hit it off. They might take a liking to each other.

If you're fortunate to have a brilliant woman in your life, by your side or as your wife, be sure to listen to her.

If You Don't Know the Old Me, You Don't Really Know Me

You can't really judge somebody unless you know their backstory. I'm not saying that you can't judge them—on the contrary, you're free to judge whoever you want to judge. And it's okay to be judged. You will be judged. But I wanted to let everybody know that if you don't know the old me, you probably don't know who I am now. I am who I am now because I was who I was then.

I don't know people as well as I think I know them. It's not a personal thing. It's not a confrontational thing, like, "Damn. You don't even know me, so you can't even say anything about me." No. I want you to remark about me, but if you don't know the old me, it's going to be hard to say that you know me. If you don't know the Gucci from Bessemer, Alabama, who was trapping at the Texaco, who was locked up again and again, who persevered to create something unique, something original, something great, then you don't really know and don't really understand the Gucci that you see today. Now, you can know me from afar. It's like me looking at other people. I know a lot of people because I followed their career. But I don't *know* them.

In this social media world, we think we see a person. But that's

just pictures, just videos. We're not with them. They're showing us what they want us to see. It's just a part of who they are. Or maybe not them at all. They could just be misrepresenting who they are. None of what they're showing us could be real. We don't know because we don't *know* them.

I've got colleagues who have become my friends. They ended up being great people. You meet somebody and they get out of jail and you're like, "Damn. That was a great friend, a great partner." They might even end up being closer to you than your own family. But then you can meet somebody when you're with that same person that has a different opinion of them because they knew them at a different point in their life, or because they grew up together. They have a different perspective, a different insight. It might be somebody who went to kindergarten with them and they've been knowing them for twenty-five years. You're thinking you know them, but you realize you didn't know things about them. Yeah, you know they're from Texas, but this person knows them a lot better than you do. You're like, "I didn't know you were adopted. Damn. I thought that was your real momma." Now you're learning more.

If we pay attention, we learn about people all the time. We all change, and we have to respect that about ourselves and each other. When we listen to people, learn their story, and understand where they are now, we can better respect their transformation, their process. We can also use that knowledge to look at ourselves and improve ourselves.

Another way to look at it is to not try and act like you know everyone. You don't. It's okay to not know everybody. It's okay to learn from somebody. That's how I feel about it. I got to this point by listening to other people, by being open. I don't know everything. I've yet to meet anybody that knows everything. My dad, he used to say that only a fool knows everything.

Protect Yourself at All Times

That is the honest truth. I have to remind myself of that. Now I'm reminding everybody about it. A lot of people, entertainers, celebrities, especially black males, say something tough, like "Ain't nobody gonna fuck with me." Or, "Don't be caught without it." It's like, no. But honestly, you've got to protect yourself at all times. Seriously. Mentally, physically, spiritually, financially.

There are bad actors. Not everyone has your interests in mind. You need to stay alert and keep yourself out of harm's way. That goes for all aspects of life. You've got to have something to live for. You've got to have something to love. You've got to have people that love you. You have to have something to protect. You've got to be a caring person to have people to care about you to a degree. You have to get to a point in your life where you're like, "I want to protect myself because I want to make it home to them." You really learn to protect yourself when you learn to protect others. When you really don't love yourself or you don't have anybody that you live for, you're a detriment to yourself.

Everybody isn't in a good space. You've got to be aware of that. We protect ourselves in so many ways. We put a fence up to keep dogs and other animals from getting into our yards. We put ourselves in a building where the elements can't come in there and freeze us to death. Sometimes you've got to protect yourself from humans, too. It's not that you've got to be scared of them, but just to protect yourself.

You've got to protect your mental space, too. You have to be confident in what you're doing. If you are strong within, you won't look for validation from the outside world. Get to a point where there are things you don't have to rely on anyone else for. If you do everything you're supposed to do, you don't need a pat on the back. That would be nice and it sure feels good. It even helps you a lot of times. But if you're really doing what you're supposed to be doing, you already patted yourself on the back, because you put the work in.

Look at my situation. I make music. When somebody asks me, "How did you make so many albums?" I say, "I went to the studio and put the time in. I recorded on the beats. I networked with a lot of producers. I invested in studio equipment. I rented space to record. I kept up with the bills. I'd teach somebody when they needed it. I ran a business. I rapped on a bunch of different beats from a bunch of different people, and people like these producers. I did a whole bunch of things. It wasn't simple. It was a challenge, and I did it for years and years. So mathematically, it was just one plus one equals two. That's what I do." Could you do it? Could it be done again? One hundred percent.

But is somebody going to do it? No. No. No. Why? They don't

want to put the work in. They're still trying to look and ask me questions instead of just doing it. I did it one day at a time. That's how I did it. That's why that Nike slogan is perfect. Just do it.

I talked to one of my closest friends and he wanted to get his big break. I told him, "Hey, there aren't any big breaks. If you aren't doing something today that's going to help you, then what are you doing?" Remember, this is my friend, my partner. I know he does a lot. He works hard, and he's a good husband, a good father. It isn't like he's lazy at all. But I told him, "The only thing I can tell you is that you've got to do more. There's no solace." He said, "Maybe I'll just get a job with benefits so I can get health care. I don't know."

I'm not saying people should do it, but you could join the army. I'm not saying I would do that, but if I had to do something other than what I do now, I would figure it out. I would do more. I'm going to squeeze everything out of what I've got going and then I'm going to try to add more to it, even if it's education. I wouldn't give a damn if I had to go to school, or do something to get a part-time job. I would keep growing with what I've got. You could throw a party once a month. You could make extra money with that. If it goes real well and you make $8,000 off that party once a month for a year, that's almost $100,000. If you're good with food, you could make money being a chef.

Just think about these things, these ideas. I'm not saying I'm a genius. But talk to someone. Brainstorm with your friends and by yourself, too. It starts small. Mobilize. But you've got to do more if you want more. There isn't any secret to it.

At the same time, you've got to take care of yourself. Let's say you're a chef. If you keep eating all the food you're cooking, your ass is going to be dead. If every time you're making red velvet cake for all these people and you're eating it, you're going to keep getting bigger and bigger. Then you realize you aren't working out. Then you start feeling it. Do you really think you're going to start working out when you're in the bed resting? When you're in there, are you going to say, "When I get up, I'm going to work out." I know what happened with my parents and my uncles.

Everybody is ready when it's too late. Protecting yourself is a full-time job. You can't wait until something goes wrong to decide you're going to change, that the time has finally come for you to do the right thing. Are you going to start when you're in a hospital bed? Now you've got all these things stuck in you, with tubes up your nose. It's easy to go have fun, to drink wine and eat some fire-ass food with all kinds of seasoning on it, with sugar and mayonnaise. That tastes good to me, too. You think I don't like it? I look at it like, "One of them has got to go. Which one?" You can't have both. You can't eat yourself into a hole and think you're going to be rewarded with good health.

If that's the mentality you adopt, no matter what you've got, you're not going to do well. It doesn't matter what state your finances are in, because you're going to die and then somebody else is going to spend your money. It doesn't matter who gets it. It could be the government, your family, your kids, your daughter, or your wife. Some people always press me with this shit. "Man. You know I'm just working because of my daughter and my son." What the fuck? So you think when you have kids, you've just got to work and that's it? That's what you were hitting it for?

That's your excuse not to advance? The society that you're born in? You aren't going to try? You don't put it on the kids? Man, that shit's weak as hell. You going to grow old like that? I don't respect that. I can't even be around people like that. But that's so common. I don't knock 'em, but I just hear them and take it in. There's a group of people that isn't going to be ready for that. I don't know them. I just want to see them from afar. They aren't going for that. That's what gave me the example to push, because you can see it. Everybody can see it. You don't have to go by what your parents showed you, what your brother showed you, what the people in your neighborhood showed you. Not at this point. All you've got to do is look in your phone if you want to be inspired. But if you don't want to do it, man, you're going to suffer that fate.

Do you want to be in the jailhouse wishing you could get back on the corner? Man, you're telling me that when you turn thirty or forty years old that you've still got to trap your way to success? That's the worst, man. I understand it. I've been there, too. That's why I tell people that you've got to squeeze the most out of what you're doing. But if you aren't parlaying that shit and you're leaving yourself out there and something happens, whatever it is, you made the choice.

Never Let Being Liked Get in the Way of Being Respected

Don't compromise your principles or your integrity just to fit in or be liked. Don't succumb to peer pressure or waver on what you stand for. Being respected is far more valuable than being liked. Not everyone is going to like you. That's just the reality.

If you stand for something meaningful, you will gain respect. And that respect will take you far. First off, find something to stand for. Once you know what you stand for, embrace it. Draw strength from it. You've got to be confident in yourself. You've got to be confident enough in yourself so that you can stand alone. You've got to be a leader, not a follower.

Humans are social animals. We want to be liked, loved, and embraced. That's just human nature. But if you are too focused on being liked, you start to make decisions that don't reflect who you are. You start trying to please people. Once you start trying to please people, you lose sight of who you are and where you're going.

Find good people to be around. You can't hang around the wrong crowd. You've got to associate with the right person, marry the right person, be in business with the right person. Find people you respect and who respect you. Find people who share your values. I know my values, and I know what I respect.

I respect dedication. I like it when I can see somebody's greatness and they don't have to tell me about it. That earns my respect. I know it took a lot of time for that person to climb that ladder. If they went so hard that they're visible to the public and I can watch it from afar, I'm not a hater. I admire that. It earns my respect when somebody just grabs ahold of something and keeps on growing.

I respect the distance they've gone. The first time I meet somebody, I don't look at how much money they've amassed or how much success they've enjoyed. I prefer to take a longer view. After ten years, you can look at that person and you're like, "Man. They're making smart moves. I like the way he carries himself. They matured. He or she evolved." Or, "Damn. I used to be like that person. Now they seem like they're in a bad place, that they went down. They fell off." I look at the evolution of the business and the person. I look at the person who went from working at one McDonald's to managing it to starting their own restaurant. I like the person who got their degree and did something with it.

These are ideas, thoughts, and things that you can actually use so that you can keep moving up. If you're a plumber, you can keep being a plumber to the point where you have a plumbing service. If you're doing hair, you might want to open a salon. If one day you have your "aha" moment that you're going to

Once you start trying to please people, you lose sight of who you are and where you're going.

own a salon, you might then say, "I'm going to own my salon by working at the barbershop for a year straight. I'm going to save my money when I can and pay my bills. I'm going to take some of this money and put it down on this spot. Eventually, I'm going to own that building. Then I'm going to sell that building." All of these things take years of dedication. I want these words to keep you going on your journey in life.

Everybody may not like you. That's to be expected. But this is America and people here respect success, even if they don't like you.

Lead by Example

People always ask me, "Gucci, why don't you go speak at schools, go to juvenile hall, or do seminars?" They feel like I should be out there all the time, shaking hands and kissing babies. Some people love doing that. I have a different way that I like to give back, though. This is my way of doing that, sharing my wisdom in this book, and making some money too. I teach through my actions every day. I'm in a position to influence, I'm in a position to lead. I lead by example. I inspire through my actions.

I don't want to be a hypocrite. Anybody can say something. But it's another category to say something and then do it. I don't follow anybody on Twitter other than my wife because I don't believe that people always do what they say they're doing. I saw Kobe doing what he was doing. I saw him working hard because he was out there competing with top-notch athletes. Anyone can see that he was dedicated to doing what he's doing.

I like the people where I can see what you're doing. You put extra hours in. You're rehearsing. You're going further than what I do. Look at Lizzo. I know that the time she put in is real. She worked for it. Anybody can say what they're going to do, but I don't see it. A lot of times I don't share stuff that I do. I tell people what I do and then they see the other part of it, the results. My whole thing is don't get distracted. So when you see me, you'll be like, "Damn. Gucci can't be distracted." The results are in front of you.

Leading by example: that is my way of publicly holding myself accountable to the world. It's not like I told everyone, "Save your money. If you're getting comfortable, you're making it easy for me." But when you see me, I better not look like I'm broke, that I'm getting comfortable and I'm cool with being fat and my suit is not fitting because I'm out there being like that. If some people want to do that, that's on them. That goes against everything that I'm about, that I stand for. They can be busted and disgusted. I can't live like that.

Let's say my buddy told me, "Hey, man. You said you were going to be on point by your birthday." Our birthdays are right by each other and he's coming down to Miami for the Super Bowl. I'm looking forward to seeing him and I don't want to hear all that nonsense from him if I fell off since we talked. When I see him, I can't have a gut. Same for him. If he keeps making promises and doesn't follow through, it'll make me not want to talk to him. It'll make me want to talk about something else. Either do what you're saying or stop saying it. Talk about your kids. Talk about your parents. Don't talk about what you're going to do and then don't make any progress toward it. Everywhere you go, you show the world who you are. Apply your self-awareness and lead by example.

Either do what you're saying or stop saying it.

In reality, most people don't want to be held accountable. Everybody wants to adopt this lackadaisical approach and hang with a bunch of people and not accept any responsibility for what they do. It's easy to do. They'd rather befriend a bunch of people who don't force them to have self-accountability for what they're doing, and then they praise them for it. They're just living in this little fairy tale their whole life. They're running from being grown. Not me. I'm running toward it. I'm trying to be the example for others to follow.

Part V

Work Ethic

Nobody Cares. Work Harder

I got these words of wisdom from Lamar Jackson, quarterback of the Baltimore Ravens. I find myself saying it in my head all the time. I always go back to it, but it can't really give you any solace. Because you've got to work hard. That's what it is. It doesn't matter if you're sore, if you're tired, if you're behind on the bills. Nobody cares. You've got to keep going. Even if you do well, do good, do the right thing, you might not get a reward. Sometimes you'll be like, "Damn, I did everything I was supposed to do and I pushed myself. Damn, I'm tired. Damn, I'm barely getting by." It's not always an enjoyable experience, but there's no need to complain about it.

Stop trying to find sympathy. It's a hard life. Nobody cares. That's why only a few people accomplish stuff they set their mind to do. It's hard to see something through, from the beginning, the middle, and the end, especially if there is no reward for all the effort.

It can start off well. But then the challenges start. You can start something off with one of your partners and you'll be excited. Then you can realize you're not on the same page. You might have to talk to them and be like, "I don't think you understand what I'm saying." Once you get past that, it'll be all for the better. But you've got to realize that sometimes you don't get past it. Life isn't a fairy tale, where difficulties come and you're able to get past them every time. No. Sometimes the storm hits and it kills people. Sometimes the war comes and there are casualties. The only people who can talk about it and write a book about it are the people that are alive, the people that woke up today.

So you have to move past the casualties. You are not one of them, because if you were one of them, you couldn't even speak on it. You're like, "Okay. If there were a bunch of casualties, the only thing you can really do is have a funeral home." Instead of saying you're broke, you know the storm is coming, so catch this. When the war is coming, some people get rich off buying war munitions. They profit off death and destruction. They say the people will govern themselves, at least with the companies that they're in cahoots with. It makes sense. Sometimes there's nothing you can do. You've got to just brace yourself.

What can I tell you if the coronavirus affects you and me? What can I tell you to help you? There's nothing I can tell you that can affect you, other than, "Hey, man. Wash your hands, stay home, and be safe." We'll have to see what the planet is going to do. What humanity is going to do. If you've been hustling enough, you can insulate yourself and quarantine yourself from people because you're not pressed to work, you're not pressed to go to school.

But what about the people who say they can't work and can't go to school? Now they're behind on their bills. Do you think their bills are going to stop? Do you think my bills are going to stop? Tragedy won't stop anything. If I didn't save for what's ahead, then whatever happens to me, honestly, I deserve it, because I worked for it but didn't plan far enough ahead.

If you fail, there may be a handful of people that really still care—if you're lucky. The other 7.8 billion people on the planet don't. So do yourself a favor and focus on yourself and work harder.

Don't Be Lazy

I've achieved a lot in my life. I'm in a position a lot of people aspire to. Sometimes you see me with my feet up on Instagram. But I'm not chilling. Laziness is not to be confused with rest.

While I was working on this book, I was working on movie scripts. You've got to stay active. Look at how one thing leads to another. You can write a book. Then somebody wants to buy the rights to that book to make it into a movie. Once you do that, now you write a second book. While you're writing your second book, your buddy says, "Let's write a movie together." The opportunities keep coming if you keep pushing yourself. Then you can still do albums. Now you're dropping albums, books, movies.

When everybody tells you that you've done something good, it can make you

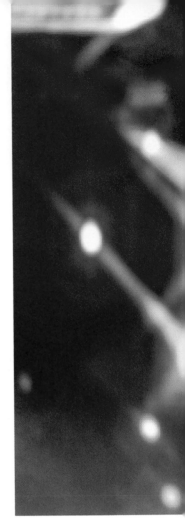

kind of lazy. It's easy to say, "Okay. That was good. I don't have to really work right now how I just worked on that, because I can take a breath. I can relax. I can enjoy that." But if you do something bad, it's like, "Damn. I know I can do better than that."

What keeps me shielded is working hard. If I do something good, I don't get caught up or get spoiled on the victory. If I get bad press or an album doesn't do the numbers I want, I keep my self-talk to, "My next one's going to be even better." I'm not going to sit around and mope and wait two years to drop something else. I get right back on it.

No matter how much you accomplish, don't be lazy. Laziness is the beginning of your end.

When They Sleep, I'm Grinding

If everybody is sleeping, that makes it easy for me. My awareness is up these days. I can see the people who are sleeping. I can see what other people are not doing, and I take advantage of that. People are content sleeping and only planning for today while I'm planning for the end, for the long game. In that equation, I'm gonna win. It will happen. Eventually, they're going to lose those opportunities and I'm going to be ready to embrace the gift.

Being sober has helped me. I don't oversleep like I used to. I'm waking up early. Changing my diet has also made a big difference. You can't change nothing if you don't change your diet. That's 100 percent. You can tell if somebody's serious by what they put in their mouth, whether that's drugs, food, whatever. The body is a temple. That's because of the comfort thing. It's like when I go on an airplane, I try to be disciplined in what I eat. They'll ask me if I want a certain drink. No. I just want water. I don't want a soda, a cranberry juice. I'll see other people on the plane say, "Let me get a drink. Let me get comfortable," even if it's a soda, a Coke and ice. All that comes from, "Let me get in the easy zone where I feel good."

But if you are content with what you've got going and what you need to handle, you don't need anything. I get on a plane, I come with a book. I sit down and I get comfortable reading the book because I already came in the zone. I'm not looking at the flight attendant. She can't really affect me. It doesn't matter if people bump me. You can't get an attitude if you already came set. I'm not saying I'm going to have a good day. I'm going to have a good year. This trip is part of my year. This is a business trip, or this is a vacation. If I'm resting, I don't have to drink a six-pack, a bottle of Cristal, a pint of lean. I'm content with just getting something to eat. I don't have to overeat anymore. I'm going to eat something I like, do something I enjoy, and get some rest.

Looking back on my day, I can say that I read a book. I went to the beach. I kicked back. I took a day to myself and I'm off to take another one. That's what I'm doing. Tomorrow I'm gonna cut my phone off. That's what I'm going to do. I'm not going to do it by accident. I'm going to let my wife know, "Hey. Tomorrow let's find us a nice restaurant to go eat. Let's be totally engaged in what we're doing right now."

I'm about focus and getting things done. So when people are distracted, sleeping, not getting things done, that's when I'm grinding.

Do More, Get More

That's the best advice that somebody can give you. Do more. Get more.

If you don't appreciate what you have, you're not going to get more. I really believe that. If you don't appreciate the car you've got and you don't keep it clean, why did you get a new car? I feel like the reason I have all the cars I have is that when I had Chevys and Regals, I was meticulous about cleaning them, about keeping them running well, about getting the oil changed.

I've been like this since I was a child, when I bought my first car. I had to go hustling to buy my own car. It was a raggedy car. I didn't think about it then, but I learned about value. I took a lot of risks in order to buy this car. I should at least keep it nice enough to where if something goes wrong, I can sell it and parlay that into another car. I would do that for years. I would go from Regal to Chevy, from Chevy to Cadillac, from Cadillac to Lexus, from Lexus to Benz. A lot of people wouldn't do that, though. Some people would just crash their car and not have any insurance and just walk away. So it'd be a total loss. But it shouldn't be that way. Just because you don't want some-thing anymore, or because you don't value it, doesn't mean that it doesn't have value or that someone else doesn't want it. Just about everything has value.

Do more. Get more. There's so much strength in those words, but there's also strength in the words we're using and you're reading now. People have told me stuff that's stuck with me and got me through some hard times. What they told me may have been from the Bible or it could have been a proverb from somebody who didn't even realize the power of what they were saying. Someone could say, "God won't put more on you than you can bear." That's wise. But only if you're alive. Somebody's had so much on them that they died of exhaustion. But I can't fret about that, because I'm here to tell it and they're not.

There's solace in these words. If you're going through a drought, you can revert to, "Hey, man. It's got to get better." Or you can say, "Okay, well, if I don't die, I guess I have to get better." We've all been at stages and points in our lives when it's painfully bad. Some people succumb to that. That's just life and death.

It's going to happen to everybody. It may not happen in a painful way. But it could. It happens to every living thing. The only thing you can do is prepare the most you can to delay it. That's evolution, survival of

the fittest. You've got to try to put yourself in the best position you can in the hierarchy physically, mentally, socially, and financially. That gives you a better chance to help your offspring out, to help your tribe, your family, your business, your race. You can't push the envelope if you're not healthy enough to push. The only thing you can do is do more.

Whatever It Is, Do It Now

As soon as I wake up, I say, "Do it now." That's the first thing I say to myself. That's what makes me jump out of bed instead of just dreading the day when I'm feeling all these aches and pains from traveling or working out. So instead of drilling down and worrying about what time things are because I've got appointments and all these things I have to do every day, I'm like, "Do it now." It gives me a head start, even if it's just to get up and wash my face and get ready for the day. It gives me an advantage. I wake up before everybody in the house, ahead of everybody else that's doing what I'm doing. It gives me that extra time, an advantage. It's pretty simple. Whatever it is, do it now.

Part VI

Opportunity

Stay Ready

When opportunity comes knocking, grab it. You've got to be ready to parlay your ventures. Five, ten years ago, I didn't seize the opportunities in front of me. I had many of the same opportunities I have now. Opportunity's been knocking. I've been having opportunities people would die for. But I took it for granted. Now, I don't take it for granted. Once you're grateful for opportunity and you respect it, you treat it as such. Now it's like, "I'm going to cuff these opportunities, and I'm going to get some more." I'm expecting stuff too, because I'm going to take care of my plan A, my day-one job. I'm going to do that to the best of my ability. I'm not taking it for granted. By me doing that so well, everybody's going to be in awe of that and then opportunities are going to come. Now I'm ready for them.

I Can Make Something Outta Nothin'

Look at me and where I'm from. In 2019, my hometown of Bessemer was named the worst Alabama city to live in by 24/7 Wall St., a financial news and opinion company. The average household income is $31,000. The violent crimes are off the chart, where there are 2,986 violent crimes per 100,000 people. The state average is 524.

I made a lot out of zero. It's super important to not let your environment define you. I apply that to my everyday life. I always think about what I do to move myself forward to be better, to advance myself. I feel like that's my answer, that I can make something out of nothing by taking a gradual approach to it, by not waiting on a big break, by doing the work, by planting the seeds, by tending the soil. Whatever it is, I'm going to be patient and continuously go about it. I can dedicate myself to it. I can overcome adversity by patience, by putting in my ten thousand hours. Even when those ten thousand hours get real hard and I've got to work a part-time job to continue to master my vocation or whatever I'm trying to do, I'm going to push through it. I'm going to be resilient. That's how I'm going to make something out of nothing. I'm not going to try to take a shortcut because there really are no shortcuts.

There's no shortcut to success, because success, ultimately, is just a word. So what I think is success, what I might think is a lot of money, you might think that is a little bit of money. I think I get a lot for a show, but that doesn't compare to what some of these younger guys get. It's always, "What's your definition of success?" But if you push me on it, my definition of success is getting the most out of what I've got—and more.

If you would have said I'd just be a teacher, okay. I'm not just going to be a teacher. I'm going to be a great teacher, then push myself to be a principal. I'll be a teacher and I'm also going to be a businessman. I'm also going to be a philanthropist and a volunteer. You can always do more.

You don't really need anything to make something happen. All you need is you. Make something.

Make Today Count

Make today count. Don't be a procrastinator. All this preparation we're talking about in this book—do it every day. As soon as you get up, think about what you did yesterday and how it fits into what you have to do today. Don't have delusions of grandeur. I named one of my albums *Delusions of Grandeur* because I always want to have a reminder for myself. There was a time when I was deluded. I put stuff off. I was feeling like I was good. I wasn't.

There's a reason we can tell when someone isn't doing what they're supposed to be doing. That's because we can look at ourselves and know what we aren't doing. But we can avoid that. We cannot just think about it. We can go every day without dealing with a problem until it catches up with us. The end is going to be painful. The descent is fast, too. It's fast and painful. We can compartmentalize and even if we see it in our loved ones, we have to pay attention to it. Even if we love them so much, we still have to pay attention.

We'll say, "I'm just thinking about the good news. I'm not going to think about the things I've seen that are deteriorating with them." You don't want to remember them for that. You don't want to say, "Damn. We could have you in your eighties if you would have made some different choices once you knew." It's hard because you can't make that decision for anybody else. We all know that. Every person struggles with it. They've got to want it. All these things I deal with, I know everybody else deals with them too.

For me, a lot of times I'll be like, "Man. That's remarkable." That's remarkable that they had the patience to put the work in. I commend someone who puts the work in, the time, because people don't want to look at that. They want to just be like, "You don't get that without it." I've seen a few people say that you can't skip any steps. That shit's so real.

Even when I look at myself and what I need and want to do, I know that I can't cheat anything. If you're cheating, you aren't achieving, because you know you're still deficient. If you go through school and they pass you and you go on and do whatever you're doing, but you can't read, you know you can't read well. So you're always going to be protective of that and not let it get exposed. That's just reality, because you can't read well. You can try to overcompensate for that by being athletic, by being slick, by being charming. There are so many other things that you can do, but you know what's going on. It may never be discovered.

You can never know how much someone does because of their talent, or whether they got to where they are because of hard work. The only people I respect are the people I see. I've got to see it. You can say, "I've seen that person in the last four or five years. Their body has developed from a skinny guy to a savage. You can tell they've been grinding." I've seen Kevin Hart go from a stand-up comedian

to an up-and-coming actor to an A-list actor. I've seen Will Smith develop from a rapper into what he's become: a successful actor on TV and an even more successful actor in the movies. He's one of the biggest stars in the world, in the history of entertainment. We all watched them do that, so you can say, "Oh, I respect them because I was privileged enough to see this progression."

But you also see child stars who grow up and crash. You see that too, so you can tell, "Damn. I can see where they have delusions of grandeur to where they thought they could do things, where they thought their superstardom made them invincible, not human." It's easy to notice someone and say, "Oh, if you take too many drugs, you'll lose your sanity. If you don't spend wisely, you'll lose all your money." It might not happen quickly, over the course of just one year. But these are the types of things you hear about. It's all that work you've got to put in, man, and doing it the right way. That's the key.

You can't stay in place. The world never stays in place, so how are we going to stay in place? How can you be like, "Okay. I'm good." Then two years from now, you're going to be good? No. You're not going to be good, man. There isn't anybody who is secure in the world, man. The world keeps spinning. We could all fall off at any time. Some freak accident shit can happen and take it all away. That's why you need to be prepared, have a backup plan, and make today count.

We all can be victims of whatever happens. It's a social world and nobody can insulate themselves anymore. Nobody. It doesn't matter how much money they have. If something happens, it affects everybody. If nobody's traveling, it affects the sports teams, the airport, Pepsi. Guess what? They own the stadium. That's what they invest in. It affects the artists. Now they can't go and do the festival at the stadium because the whole country was under quarantine. The shit gets real. I tell you all the stories for a reason.

You've got to make every day count. That's why I keep saying that it's a delusion of grandeur that you're good. No. You aren't good. Now if they say that the healthiest people can survive something, you're not even in that percentage. You can't help that it came when you were sixty years old, sixty-five years old. But what you can help is being healthy enough to where you're in the upper echelon of sixty-five-year-olds so it won't affect you. You're the picture of health.

But you'll never see somebody if they catch something and they're gone. You can't blame anybody else for that. That's why you've got to make every day count. You had to make that day count years ago. You've got to say, "This is the day I take control of my finances." You could've made that decision ten years ago and been on the journey toward that because you still would have gotten to your destination. It's still life. Every day is still going to count. The only thing that would have changed is that you would have put yourself in the best situation you can. Or not.

You can settle for mediocrity like most of the population, if you're cool with that. Remember, what I think is average you might think is superb. Things that I used to think are superb, now I think they're average. That growth came from me keeping my principles front of mind. Do it now. Make today count. Keep improving. Don't be lazy. Everybody must be held accountable.

It's like the more I do, the more I demand of myself. But I understand that too. This is how I look at rapping. The more I rap, the more I want my rappers to be bigger. I want to be better. If I make today count, I will be better tomorrow.

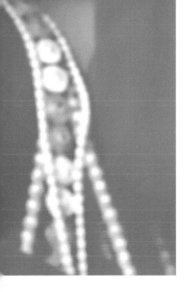

I Turn Burdens into Blessings

You don't have anything but what life gives you. You can be born into abject poverty or great wealth. That's not up to you. Life is a burden. You can cry about it or you can use it to your advantage. What feels like a burden at first might just be a challenge. I'm not trying to make this into a self-help thing and I'm not saying burdens aren't real, but no burden lasts forever. No burden is un-changeable. It's temporary. You got to do things to make it better.

Whatever you can do—have faith, and hope that things are going to improve. You have to do the thing for it to improve. Ac-cepting that process—that's when you've really got faith. Any time I encounter a hard-ship or a burden, I make it into a challenge and that challenge becomes a blessing, an opportunity for growth. If you look at ev-

159

erything as an opportunity, how are things not going to improve? Two and two has got to equal four.

Imagine if you put yourself in a situation where your health went all the way down. You can do some things to make it come back, but you can also do things to not make your health deteriorate. If you didn't say anything about that part, then the hell with it. Straight up. People will be like, "My buddy just had a stroke." Do you think he just got up and got sick that day? Do you think you're going to eat and drink all this shit until you have a stroke and you're saying, "Fuck it?" It's sad. So you're telling me that God didn't send you a sign that that is killing you? Okay. Come on. You didn't know that you were falling asleep on the couch every day, or that you can't walk. It didn't matter then? But it matters now?

For me, I'm going to take care of myself. I'm not doing this shit for fun. I'm doing it because it's the responsible thing to do. I also feel like if you have a wife and you have a family, you are responsible to take care of your health and be there for them. You can't just be like, "Fuck it. I'm just going to eat and drink myself to death."

How are you telling me that you're going to take care of your family and it's going to expand, but you're tricking off all the money? That doesn't go together. Or you're telling me that you're going to open up a business and you've got this, that, and the third. You need to take care of your life. That's what you need to do. Then everything else will fall into place because you do one thing how you do everything.

That's one way I can tell if someone isn't serious, especially about finances. You have to realize that how you do one thing is how you do everything. That's one of the biggest quotes there is. You can look at an athlete and tell if they're in shape, if they're not, if they've been training. Some people are born with talent and then it just deteriorates. Some people hit the lottery and they get a big lump sum. Then it breaks down. Sometimes people are born with a silver spoon, which is not bad. Their people had money and they

passed it down. They either blow it, or sometimes they get crafty, expand it, and make it bigger.

You are either going to do something or you aren't going to do it. That's what I'm basically saying. You've got to decide what kind of person you're going to be. We all have our circumstances that could be looked at negatively or positively. You have to take anything you deem negative and flip it so that it helps you in some way. You have to have that motivation if you want to truly be great. You gotta take that journey, make that change. Once you do, though, you have to stay at it. You don't want to lose that blessing.

It isn't like you work out and you get in shape and then it's over. No. That's what people don't understand. You work out and you do that until you die. The body is a metaphor for life. It takes constant tending to. Now, instead of a dying at sixty you can stay alive to ninety and be in good shape. The longer that you don't do it, the bigger hole you dig. We're all going to deteriorate and die like any other animal. But you can prolong life, learn, grow, and evolve. That's all we've got. Period. What choice are you going to make? Are you going to put it somewhere in your mind where you just don't deal with it? You can say, "It's not like it's in front of me and I'm going to die tomorrow. I'm not going to catch a heart attack tomorrow if I eat this steak and hamburger. If I quit my job, it's not going to affect me directly today."

Okay. You quit your job now, but a year from now it's going to have terrible consequences. If you start today and just drink a beer a day and then some days two beers and stop exercising right now, your health is going to decline slowly. It's going to start showing and then people are going to be like, "Since when did you not start taking care of yourself?" At first it creeps up slowly. But after a while you realize how far behind you fell. The good thing is that you can stay in front of it. That's a choice to make. Do you want to be employed fifty-two weeks out of the year? That's a choice. That's what an aware person knows. But another person will be like, "Hey, man.

I'm chasing my dream. I not going for a nine-to-five." Or, they'll say, "I'm going to take out a loan. I'm gonna go to school." That might be a good decision, or it could be a bad one depending on the passion of that person.

How serious are they about what they're trying to do? Some people feel like they go to school and that's all they've got to do. But they're partying, kicking it, having fun, going back and forth to home, and learning. You can go to school now and work and raise a child. That's what my momma did. She raised a child, went to school, graduated, and worked two, three jobs. My momma, she was all-in to provide for us. She didn't treat us like burdens, even though I was one at times. I look at every burden, every responsibility, as an opportunity to provide a blessing for myself and my family, just like my momma did.

Part VII

Success

Whatever You're Thinking, Think Bigger

Imagine your life today, tomorrow, ten years from now. Do you want to have a gold single? Why not have a multi-platinum album? You want to have a barbershop? Why not try to have a national chain? You want to be a doctor? Aim to be surgeon general. Whatever you see, multiply it. That's how you grow. Whatever it is, think bigger.

I got in this because I knew myself. I trusted myself. I knew from a young age what I was after. Then, I tried to think bigger. Even though I made my first recording when I was twenty-one, twenty-two, right after I had gotten my first charge, I made the decision to try something different, something new. I knew that I had that dog in me. I knew that when I put my head down toward something, whether it was hustling or saving money, I was responsible enough that, whatever it is, once I say I was gonna do it, I was going to do it. I didn't want to let myself down. That's the only thing that scared me.

Once I say I'm going to do it, it is by any means necessary. It wasn't for the love of the music. It was for the love of the entrepreneurial spirit. Sure, I love making music. But rap, that was going to be the vehicle to get me there. I'm not comfortable with being average. I want to say I've done this. If somebody said real estate was going to be it, I was going to be the best black real estate agent. I would show that even though I was from humble beginnings, I could do this. Whatever it was, I knew I was going to get there. If it was producing, I would have learned how to make the beats.

Once I put my mind to getting in the music game, I knew I couldn't catch another charge. Even when I got back in the streets, I was like, "Okay. Now I'm going to use the streets to make sure that this music shit works." I was going to apply what I knew about the streets, and what people in the streets liked, to make my music work. They like reality raps, to hear about what's really going on in the hood, on the block. That's what I was doing. I was an expert at that, so that's what I rapped about. It was a means to an end. I came in with a CEO mentality. I wanted to be rich. Thinking big keeps me going.

I'm Cut from a Different Cloth

I feel like I'm one of those one percenters you rarely come across. I wasn't born with a silver spoon. Both of my parents came up dirt-poor. My beginnings were super humble. 1017 First Avenue, Bessemer, Alabama. Where I came from to where I am—I did a lot with what I had, which wasn't much. I knew I had to approach life differently.

I'm cut from a different cloth. That mantra steers me. It's a general mindset that allowed me to blossom. If I could only sell five thousand copies of one of my projects, I was going to parlay that so that I could get the most out of it. I pushed the talent I had as far as anybody could push it. I feel like I'm the five-foot-eleven dude that made it to the NBA. I did it off sheer determination. If my career should've been three years, I parlayed it into fifteen.

I do consider myself an elite artist and an elite talent and the best ever. But at the same time, my numbers don't show that I sold fifteen million or ten million. People are like, "Why do you say you're the GOAT?" Man, that shit don't matter to me. I don't get any money for that. I don't want to see anybody arguing over that if they don't have any money. I'm the GOAT because how did I end up with more than a lot of the other people out there? They don't have any grind.

I look at somebody like a JT the Bigga Figga or a Master P. I looked at JT as somebody who said, "I'm going to get my mine some kind of way." Then you can look at somebody like a Tech N9ne. He was like, "Whatever it is that I've got, I'm going to make the most out of it. If I have to go independent and just sell merch, go on the road and that's the vehicle I have to use, then that's what I'm doing." Like me, those types of artists always adapt. I've just got to get there. There isn't even any doubt about it.

When I was young, I saw people getting money. It was a competition to see who was getting the most money. It wasn't like, "Gucci's getting money in the hood and nobody else is getting money." Nah. Everybody in my neighborhood was getting money. Everybody in my city was getting money. So it was like, "Who's the richest on this street? Who's the richest in this neighborhood? Who's the richest in my zone? Who's the richest on this side? Who's the richest in the city?"

Those were my thoughts and my crew's thoughts. That's what we talked about, but everybody wasn't on that. Everybody wasn't saying, "Hey. We want to be so fresh at sixteen that we can get into the eighteen-and-over club." But we still wanted to go to the teen club and be fresh there and look like we're eighteen.

"You've got to use your head for more than a hat rack."

But it took money. It took drug selling. That's the backstory. That popularity gave me the drive to keep having the money to feed this monster I created. I got lucky. It doesn't always end well.

But I was smart the whole time. I was always so rough with my friends. I got that from my dad. I would say, "You've got to use your head for more than a hat rack." My daddy would always tell me that because I would put my hat on backward. He would tell me that I had to think. I thought I was so slick and so cool, but I wasn't being smart. All my friends would think what my daddy said was so smart and cool, but they would be dumb.

He was like, "No. You don't have to be dumb to be street. You can be street. You can be vicious. You can be rough. You can

be tough. You can be cool. But at the same time, you need to know how to act. You need to know how to read the menu when we go out. If you can't, that isn't funny." These are the things that separated me.

Prepare Yourself to Be Successful

When you are prepared, you kind of work in silence. You've got this earnest, true confidence and you're not being fake. You don't need to make noise. You are attracting success with your preparedness. Like the young boys say, "There's no cap on it." There's no need to try to sell anybody on anything. When you show up, people know who you are because you already did the work and you're ready to work. You really don't need to say anything because you're prepared.

Have you ever watched two fighters and just watched their body language? I like to watch old classic fights. I like to see how they come into the ring. You can tell who's prepared and who's scared. It's not that the other person is not trying. It's just that the other person has trained more. They've laid the groundwork for success. They're prepared to win.

When Mike Tyson was in his prime, you could tell that his opponents were scared even before they got in the ring. They hadn't trained as well as Mike. The times he did lose, it was always to athletes who were in super-great condition. I'm talking about they looked like they could be bodybuilders, that they shouldn't even fight. If you think about Evander Holyfield and Lennox Lewis, they looked unreal. It was like when the Golden State Warriors were on top and people said they didn't get a game off, that they always had to play their best. That's how other boxers were approaching Tyson. Once he got comfortable and the other person was training out of control for the next six or seven months leading up to the fight, the challenger now has the advantage. He's accumulated the interest. That works for bad habits, too. Tyson's bad habits had accumulated, too. He had beat five, six tomato cans in a row and he didn't really have to train that hard. Now you've fought somebody who fought five or six guys in a row who were tough opponents and he's been training hard. So now you meet the wrong person on the wrong day. Then you look at Floyd Mayweather. He's training constantly, so whenever you catch him, you catch him at his best. He's never falling off.

Mayweather didn't take a fight and then go get drunk. He didn't put poison into his lungs, his body, his organs. That would have just made it so he has to get back into shape. He stays in shape. The best fighters, you could take them from the boxing ring and they could play running back, point guard, tennis. Whatever you wanted them to do. They were prepared.

A partner of mine would always say that the better-conditioned athlete will win. He was a fifty-year-old bodyguard and used to beat all the young boys playing basketball. They weren't in shape. Yeah, they might be young, but they're smoking blunts and drinking lean.

178

He's not doing that. He's living well, working out every day, and jogging with boots on. He'd been in the army. He knew how to keep his body in shape. So all he had to do was be physical with them and he would win.

Look at Baltimore Ravens quarterback Lamar Jackson. In the fourth quarter, he's still running by everybody because they're tired and he's not. When you've got confidence like that, you try different stuff. You start thinking and playing like, "I don't care. I'm going to run and spin because I'm confident my body can do this."

I ain't tiptoeing through the hole because I'm scared, like, "Damn. If they hit me, they're going to kill me. No. I'm feeling in great shape. My body feels good. I'm feeling strong and invincible. I'm not worried. I'm going straight up through the hole. I'm going to jump over everybody. Even if I'm going to land on the ground, I know I'm going to bounce back. I'm confident in that. I can take that."

You're either going to be the Mike Tyson who's trained and ready, or you're going to be the guy who's scared because he knows his opponent trained harder. On top of that, that other person may or may not have more God-given abilities than you. They may be taller than you or just more naturally athletic. They may have more resources than you. Maybe their daddy put them through camp, private school, academy. All that comes into play.

You've got to always put yourself in the best position to win. Period. That's all you've got. Or you're going to complain about it. But that's not going to help. Instead of worrying about things, I think about how to fix them.

When I was a little boy, I would tell myself, "I stay in Georgia by myself. Man, I don't have any family here." People would say to me, "Why are you going anywhere? You're so dirty." Looking back at it now, I wasn't dirty. It was kind of a Machiavellian approach to life. I was like, "I got to get right. I don't have any extended family here, but I've got hella extended family back in Alabama. But how in the world is that going to help me here?"

So if my momma's at work and my dad is in jail and my brother's at work, who am I going to call if I get into trouble? I've got to make smarter decisions. If I get locked up right now, nobody's going to be able to come get me before they get off of work. Things like that will influence what you do because I don't have an auntie to call. But people in my neighborhood, they can take all type of chances because they've got a network of people to help them. But when I went back to Alabama, I was way more comfortable, man. I could drink, do more things. It was a more relaxed environment because I had more people there.

Life is just what you make it. When I was a little boy, I used to be jealous of the dope boys in the hood. Their mom and dad would let them sell dope and I'm like, "I've got to hide my stash from my momma." My mom was a good parent, but I was like, "This is giving them an unfair advantage. They're driving Lexuses. I'm hustling harder than them and I've got more balls than them, but I'm in a Chevy and it's a piece of junk. I've got to keep getting it fixed. My mom isn't down with what I'm doing." In my mind back then, I used to be livid. I was like, "Man, these dudes got a cakewalk." Some of their brothers dealt drugs. Some of their daddys and mommas were hustling. I didn't have any plugs. I had to get the work and break it down myself. It wasn't glamorous.

But I would see those dudes, man, living the good life. I'm like, "I gotta be in this run-down hotel." I knew the risk. I knew the reward was high, but the risk was high, too. I was like, "They can sell dope out of their house." Their mom was spoiling them. These were my *friends*. I could go down and smoke a blunt with them when their people went out. Man, I couldn't do shit like that in my house in seventh, eighth grade. I had to hide my beeper. My mom was like, "What the fuck you got a beeper for? And who the fuck is beeping you? And where are you going?"

You've got to make a way. I didn't let anything deter me. I knew I had to prepare myself, and I was determined to.

Even though these things were going on, it took so much energy to keep that stuff secret. I also couldn't do everything I wanted to do, because I had to go to school. Then I couldn't just slack off in school. I had to at least maintain some kind of presence in school. There was a lot to it.

Prepare first, success second. You've got to make a way. I didn't let anything deter me. I knew I had to prepare myself, and I was determined to.

Relax, but Don't Get Comfortable

Never get too comfortable, man. Period. You have to look at all aspects of your life and make sure you're not slacking. Are you too comfortable with your routine? Your relationship? Your kids? Your diet? Your money? When you are, you can get caught slipping. Know when to relax. But never get comfortable.

Part of not being comfortable is always pushing yourself to be better. Look at me. I can take guidance because I know what I don't know. That's how I'm able to learn. This is why I'm so good at grabbing proverbs and being a sponge. But at the same time, you have to have a foundation of knowledge for me to listen to you.

There's always another level that you can get to. There's a broke person. Then there's a person who has something. Then there's a person who can tell you what they have. So this is the person who could tell me where they got it, who isn't chasing anything but wants to help people. There are so many different levels. First you're struggling. Then you get kind of stable. Once you get stable, eventually you want to get to a point where you are doing well. You want to go from being a sponge to the point where you're releasing, to where you have something to give. Now you're a philanthropist, basically.

Once you get to a point where you're so successful that you're like a Bill Gates or a Warren Buffett, they give away a lot of the stuff they have, whether it is money or knowledge. They're like, "I understand that my legacy is secure. I'm going to be a benefit for as many people as I can with the resources I have because once I'm gone, who knows what they're going to do with these resources. So before I go, let me put something toward these causes that I've got a passion for and that can give me a tax write-off at the same time." They have everything and they're not even comfortable with that. They decided to give things away. That's how they got some comfort.

That's why it's important to understand that everything evolves and you have to learn to not take things personally. You may get to the point where you think somebody is doing something vicious to you. It's almost like nothing is vicious. Not to say that nothing is evil and nothing is painful and nothing is dangerous or vindictive. But once you start understanding the truth that everybody's got their own interests and agenda, and that that's where they operate from, you'll see that everything on the planet doesn't revolve around you. Somebody may do something hurtful or bad to you even though they're not mad at you. They may just do it.

Never get too comfortable, man. Period.

It's like a mosquito when it bites you. It hurts, but it doesn't bite you because it's personal. It's a mosquito. That's what they do. They bite people. People who hurt do hurtful things, but at the same time, people are trying to eat. So if you wonder, "Why is he overshadowing me to show more favor to his nephew?" he's taking care of his family. That's why. Pure and simple. He might have to put some paint on it because it's a job that he doesn't own. Now, he might not own Pepsi, so he uses his influence to influence the hierarchy at his job, socially. It's the same thing animals do. They look out for their own first. At the end of the day, it's just evolution.

I think about that when I think about myself and my family. My dad told me a lot of things that influenced me and that hurt me when he said them to me. But guess what?

When he said them, I could only understand them at the level I was at when he said them to me. He can only give it to me from the game that he got from the '70s, '80s, '90s. But once you mature, you can understand things better. A lot of people, though, never get to have that depth, that level of intelligence to be able to see that.

Because it takes a lot to be self-aware like that. I'm not even saying you have to be the deepest brother or the smartest person. But for you to have the self skills to say, "Hey. I can't blame my parents. They did what they could do with what they had. Whatever knowledge they had, they gave it to me."

I had partners of mine in the same apartments, a couple of buildings down, their mother was on crack. My mother wasn't on crack. But if that was the case, what could I have done about it? What could my partners have done? Now that we're older, some of them are still my partners. They either overcome it or they get overcome *by* it.

It's remarkable. It's tragic. It's amazing. You can be an underdog story or you can be a story where they're like, "Damn. This is the reason he went down the wrong path." Everything has a story behind it. But if you can make something out of nothing, you've got to be dedicated. You've got to say, "Hey, listen. If the odds are stacked against me to where I'm fifty steps behind everyone else, then I'm going to have to take fifty steps forward and pray and hope that I get to where I'm going. Even the prayer, maybe it'll give me a little solace." You put in the work and you get those fifty steps. Now you're on a level playing field with everyone else. I can take fifty or more steps to where I will advance myself so I can help my family. From there, I can help my son and help my daughter. That's it. That's life. If you were a slave during the '80s, the '90s, guess what? You're dead. I hope you passed your children something.

Once you get an understanding of how life is, you'll see that it doesn't matter if things are good or bad. What matters is what you're going to do about it. You've still got to get something to eat at the end of the day. I know things are messed up and people keep doing things that are dirty. I'm not overlooking that. I'm not saying that I'm not conscious of it. I'm not saying it's not messed up.

I'm also not saying what are *we* going to do about it? I'm saying what are *you* going to do about it? You personally. Every individual. That's what my book is for. It's like, "Hey, this is what you need to do first."

Don't be that person who says, "Damn. We could have won the Super Bowl if we didn't throw that interception." Have you ever had anybody say some shit like that to you before? They're like, "Bruh. If they didn't fumble, we would have won." Come on, man. Now that I'm grown, when people talk like that to me, I just don't even want to hear it. It's like, "Man. You had three hours to win that game. It wasn't one play." You forgot about all the other stuff that happened, right? Old boy dropped how many passes? What about the personal foul when old buddy just spit on the dude? We aren't going to talk about that, right? What about the coach not managing the game right? He's just stupid as hell. That doesn't come up either. It wasn't noteworthy.

People wake up and are like, "Damn. I need a hip replacement. My knee went out." You forgot that you overate every day. Now you're obese. That's on you. It's the same thing as the game. You're just talking about the interception or your knee or your hip, but you're not talking about the eighty sandwiches you ate. You're not thinking about that. Or you're not talking about the eighty times that you worked out and what you feel like. Guess what? Now you've got strong hips and knees because you didn't get comfortable being overweight. You did something about it.

You've got to be dead serious when you wake up and look at your day. You've got to be serious about the way you live your life.

I Don't Do Things for Fun

This is something my daddy used to say. If you think about it, it's real. I said to him one time, "Let's play cards for fun," because I had lost my money to him. He showed me how to play for a dime, maybe a dollar. He taught me for like a month. Then when it was over with, I was like, "Give me my money back." Now this was around the same time he said, "You quit when you win." I was like, "Why'd you quit on me?" He was like, "If I don't quit when I win, when am I going to quit?" So he was really giving me a lot of game. So I said, "Dad. Let's just play for fun. I know how to play now." He said, "I don't do things for fun. We need to gamble or not do it, because the last time I did something for fun, I had a son."

I was just a little boy from Alabama sitting with my dad. That was like some instructions *then*. It went over my head. I was like, "You had fun with my momma?" I was like, "What in the world?" Even though that's my dad, you don't say that to me, dog. Now I look at what he's saying. It's ruthless. He was like, "I don't really play. I just gave you your money back. The game's over. I'm through playing. Go play." I was like, "Damn." But you see I still remember it and he told me that when I was nine. I'll never forget that.

It was 1989 and we were in the Mountain Park Apartments. I always rap about them. It was when I moved with my dad from Alabama to Georgia. He was showing me how to play cards. I had two homeboys I had met in those apartments. We started gambling from there. That's how we started being friends. It was ironic, because as soon as we got the apartment, like two weeks later, the bounty hunters came and got my dad from the house and locked him up. I'm like, "This stuff is crazy. They took my dad and locked him up." But they weren't the police. They knocked the door down. They had handcuffs and a badge around their neck.

My dad called home from Fulton County Jail and I'll never forget accepting that collect call. He said, "Let me speak to your momma." I said, "Daddy. What happened? The man came and got you." You know what he said? "Oh, no. Those were my high school buddies. They were playing a practical joke on me." So I said, "What?" Now remember, they didn't have any police cars out there. They might have had a Lincoln Town Car, or some shit like that. I said, "Thanks for calling, Dad." You know I called my dad Gucci, so I told my mom, "Gucci said they played a practical joke on him, his friends from high school." She said, "Oh. That's what he said?" She just went on with it. It took three, maybe six months in the neighborhood, people were like, "Why they'd lock your dad up?" I was like, "Nah. That was a practical joke." Then they put me up on game. I was like, "Man. Things are kind of different up here."

Of course you've got to have some fun and enjoy yourself. What's crazy, though, is that I usually end up getting some sort of benefit when I take a moment to do what I thought was just going to be fun, something I just thought I would enjoy. Like earlier this year I watched the *Dolemite Is My Name* movie with Eddie Murphy. We've got a very similar story, because my thing was like I almost had to invent a character. Even though they called me Gucci when I was younger, I didn't like that. That was my daddy's name. So when people would call me Gucci, I would rebel against that name. I wouldn't tell a girl my name was Gucci. I would say my name was something else because I looked at Gucci as a family nickname. So as I got caught up selling dope and I felt like this was going to be my career, as far as being an executive or in rap, I said, "I'm going to use my daddy's name, Gucci Mane." I really didn't know how to rap, so I used all this game that I've been given from him and his friends. I'd been hearing how they talked, and they were slick. I was grown now and I was like, "I can do this myself," instead of putting my money into somebody. That was the basis of me rapping. It wasn't a game. It wasn't for fun.

My first song was "Lawnmower Man" and the chorus was something my daddy would always say: "Don't let your mouth write a check that your ass can't cash. I'm the lawnmower man and your ass is grass." That means I'm gonna beat your ass when I come home. He never whooped me, but that would just be a threat. He would say that, and then say he was going to take me in the back.

It was stuff like that, things people tell you to stop you from talking back. So in my first song, that was the hook. To everybody else, they were like, "That's the slickest thing I ever heard." I used to think that too, the first time he told me that. I took some of the stuff that they were saying. I was already in the streets, so it was just like, "Wow. I'm gonna put this in there. Nobody else is saying this type of thing, at least not on wax." Even now, a lot of the stuff that I use in my songs, I've been hearing for years and years. It's just that everybody ain't hip to it.

That speaks to the value of listening. God blessed you with two ears and one mouth so you can listen twice as much as you talk. That ties into something else my daddy taught me about playing cards: whoever's broke starts talking junk. He was like, "I can tell you who lost out here because whoever has the emptiest pocket is making the most noise. If they're driving a wagon and they're coming down the street, they can't stay on the road. They're jumping around, making that clink, clink, clink sound. If you've got something in the wagon, it just goes down the road smoothly. You won't hear it talking."

So now that applies to me now. People are like, "Why'd you change your demeanor?" I've got more money. I'm way more calm. Life is way smoother. But when I didn't have it, I made a lot more noise coming down the road. I wanted everybody to hear me. What my daddy was telling me didn't make sense then. It makes sense now. When you see a bunch of people, the loudest ones are usually the ones that don't have anything going on. They're the ones that want to start a mess. Everybody that's got something going on, they're calm. They're respectful and nice.

These words, these proverbs are important. Dolemite would use them. Ice Cube used them for his song titles. Even look at Jesus in the Bible. He talks in proverbs because it's a simple way to communicate to the masses. It's not like Ice Cube or Dolemite or rock 'n' roll "invented" them. This is just the history of the world. Some people are just not aware. I am. That's why by applying these things to my life, I can just do things over and over. That's why I can do 103 albums or somebody can write 3,500 articles. The difference is, I know how to work it and get paid for it. Everybody else around here is just goofing off.

I'm serious with mine. It's not a game. I can have fun later.

God blessed you with two ears and one mouth so you can listen twice as much as you talk.

Learn to Compartmentalize

You've got to learn how to compartmentalize your life. It all starts with your mind. Your mind is your main organizational tool. You have to use it to manage your time and your emotional and physical energy. I know when I'll be performing, so I know I have to focus on what I need to do before I hit the stage. I ain't thinking about other life shit. Compartmentalizing allows me to conserve my energy and allocate the right mental and physical resources to every task I need to do.

You can have enough energy and plan your day to spend the rest of the evening in the studio. Or you can go to sleep earlier and you can do more at the beginning of the day. It's all about what is more efficient for you. Or you can not compartmentalize and live in your mind and kind of let the wind blow you. You let life totally dictate what happens. You can say, "Okay. Opportunity came today. Opportunity didn't come today. I went to the club last night so I overslept today." You've got a sporadic, nomadic kind of lifestyle. But you don't have to do that. It's all in your mind.

Somebody could say, "What's up? You want to go out for lunch?" You'll be like, "Man. I stayed out all night." People will call me and be like, "I called you last night." I'll be like, "Yeah. I was asleep. I'm planning on going to the gym because I've got a trainer. It's business and I've got to pay him in advance. I've got to be here on his time, so if I stay out and don't do the workout, what in the world am I giving him this money for?"

Certain things don't make sense, but I didn't have to make that schedule. I'm not a slave to that schedule. I'm conscious of all the decisions that I make. At the same time, I'm not saying that I'm the sharpest person in the world. I'm just saying I'm trying to stand in front of it and present these lessons to people. I read books. I try to keep the right people around me to keep me on track, to keep me going forward. If the people that mess with me could start putting that in their skill set, I know it would help them.

Being in prison, that's when I got started reading. Everybody's reading because you've got nowhere to go, nothing to do.

So you read to pass time and of course you learn a bunch of information from books. Not saying that I've always been the biggest reader, but since I was a little boy, I knew how to read and write, so those are things that I was never ashamed to do. I always thought you should be able to go to a book or an encyclopedia if you wanted to know something. Before you could just Google it, I would try to find out myself and search it myself. I would look in the phone book. I feel like I've been using that tool since I was a child. It's a part of life. But to people who were essentially illiterate, it would amaze them. They'd be like, "Damn. When did you take up reading?" I was like, "It's in me. It's important to us all." I write out my raps, so reading and rapping have been important to me since day one.

I need to tend to my body, my marriage, my family, my mind. I have to compartmentalize to be the best I can be for every one of those things.

Now I know that I have to take care of the different compartments of myself. I need to tend to my body, my marriage, my family, my mind. I have to compartmentalize to be the best I can be for every one of those things.

Fuck Everybody, Stack Your Bread

People are like, "Damn, Gucci. How did you get this deal? How you do this? How in the world do you do this?" I just keep fucking going. I keep fucking going. I keep stacking. I handle everything every day. Everything that I did last year, I still got it. Nobody else has it. I see some people that no matter how well they do, all their money's gone next year. They've still got their fame, but they've lost all their money and a lot of their relationships. But they're still hot. I'm not wishing that anyone would sizzle down, but nobody can go on forever.

Ultimately, it's going to come to a point where, "What do you have? What do you have in your war chest?" I'm like, "I've got to get my war chest up." Everybody else is all over the place. So guess what? That's my compounding interest. That's my advantage, and I didn't share. It's not like I was telling it to the world. Before Twitter and before this book, I was in the dark doing it. My Twitter following is way different than my Instagram following. People on Twitter may not even be on Instagram. It's totally different people. People on Instagram, they see that part of my life and have been knowing me since I changed. But there's people just now getting on Gucci. They just know this positive Gucci. But to me, this is what I've been on. But now people are like, "He's dead-ass serious." I'm not going to stop. While y'all are stopping, I'm growing. That's my way of putting it out there, on Twitter. It's almost like a mantra, like self-talk. Once you stop seeing it, it means that I'm not going well. So, it can't ever stop.

I had unique skills that separated me from people in my field. But I couldn't always take full advantage of them. I would take advantage and then I would reward myself. So I would put out a project and then I would be irresponsible and wouldn't be available for my partners that I put the project out with. I was doing shows and I wasn't consistent. Now, I'm more consistent, more conscious. I learned how to keep stacking.

Life isn't about one moment. It's about a series of them. Do your best to make the most of those moments so that you're prepared for the next one. Keep stacking. That's it. Whatever it is. Find that joy, that happiness. At the end of the day, fuck everybody, keep stacking.

Part VIII

The Power of Love

I Love My Wife

Marriage is one of the best things that ever happened to me. My wife makes me so happy. I found a great wife, a supportive wife, a wife with an income who helps me, a wife who was already financially literate and had skills she could help me with. She challenges me to get better. She holds me accountable, too, when I share stuff with her and say, "Hey. Here's what I'm gonna do. I'm going to try to put out a better album, get in better shape, watch what I eat and what I say."

I know I've got somebody who can set me straight. She can be like, "I know you want to watch what you eat, but then every day you want to go out to eat." She checks me and says, "Damn. You said you were going to the trainer, but come on, Gucci. I haven't seen you go to the gym." She's somebody that's doing something. We had similar paths to greatness. She's self-made. It's not like we're just married. It's not like I was trying to find a wife to help me. But in a lot of ways, my wife is my secret weapon. If I'm going to be traveling for a long time, she might help me with that so that it's efficient and I get the most out of it. That gives me more time to do something else. So now the trip goes even better. I don't make her cook and pack, she cooks and I pack. It's good to have somebody that isn't a hindrance. She's only been a help.

I noticed these things immediately. We fell for each other fast. The more I discover about her the harder I fall. But I definitely wasn't ready for marriage. I wasn't thinking about marriage, but I saw traits in her that made us work together. That's what attracted me to her more than the physical. Once I started talking to her, it wasn't hard to see that she's smart and she's driven. She started sharing more and more of herself, and it made me see that she was different and special. But it took me a bit of maturing. We met in 2010. It took me until 2013 before I was in the headspace where I was thinking about sharing our lives together. I had to wise up and become a more responsible person so that our relationship would stand the test of time.

By the time I got serious about her, we had broken up and got back together. I

needed somebody. When I was locked up I would reach out to her and she would be there for me, just on a friend level. When I came back to her like, "I want to marry you. I know what kind of woman you are," and that I needed her, she didn't reject me, but she straight-up said, "You've got to prioritize. You need to focus on your career and focus on your health." She said, "Get a piece of paper and write it down. First thing is your family, your little boy. Focus on getting that taken care of while you're in there. Secondly, your career." We went down the list. She said, "When you get all that together, everything else will fall in place."

So it wasn't like a rejection. My life was all over the place and it wouldn't have worked at that point. You've got to have a foundation. My wife knew what the building blocks are for a marriage—a rock-solid marriage—and I didn't. I had to listen to her. When I did, when I really took the time to concentrate and create those building blocks, everything worked.

My wife stood by me through thick and thin. Every day I'm grateful for her. I love my wife.

I Told My Wife Her Presence Is the Present

One thing I heard somebody say, man, and this is the realest thing I ever heard: no matter how much you love a woman, she's going to love you more. You can't outdo it. It doesn't compare. I value her endlessly, but she's going to do *whatever* for me. Knowing that, I never want to disrespect her. Even if I might be human and slip sometimes, I love her. I'm going to love her when she isn't around, because she's doing it for me when I'm not around. She is a gift and her presence is the present.

I have got to go that extra step for her because that's what I want somebody to do for me. I don't want somebody that is only there for me when I'm around. I need somebody who's got my back when I'm not there. When you aren't in their presence, they're making sure you're straight. They're thinking about you because at the end of the day, they're like, "Gucci's going to come home." I keep a lot of things in mind, man. I don't want my wife to get hurt. That guides me if I think I'm off the path. She's doing things where it's like, "I thought this was best for you." I know that because when I talk to her, it comes out.

I didn't think that I was going to get married. I had certain criteria.

I always felt like I was intelligent. I was blessed that I always worked hard at whatever I did, but I was always encouraged to be smart. My mother was a schoolteacher, especially when I was in Alabama. I felt that if I got married, I should be well off. I'm not going to get married unless I'm rich. Even when I had a serious girlfriend, I would say I didn't want to get married because everybody gets divorced. They jump out there. They do too much and then they get divorced. Dude gets married, gets a truck. They get a house. He starts working more hours. She gets out of shape. He starts being resentful. I started seeing that with my whole family. Even if they stayed together, it wasn't a life I wanted to live. All the people I knew that were still together, they didn't have the relationship that I wanted.

I also grew up listening to music where the rappers would be like, "Bitches ain't shit but hoes and tricks." "Fuck them hoes." "Gold-digging bitch." That influenced me. When I was eighteen, nineteen, twenty, I was like, "Fuck that ho." That's how I felt for real. It wasn't like I was in school, going to college, and having long-term girlfriends. It was almost like I had girlfriends and in my mind I was like, "I'm never going to have a baby by her, though. I'm not trying to get married to her."

I grew up though. Once I got in my thirties, I was like, "Okay. Can I get my life to a point where I've got enough money to where I feel like I'll never go broke? Can I maintain what I've got going on and have a wife, and learn the skills to keep this going?" I knew it was going to take being sharp as hell. That's the only way I'm going to be a plus to anybody. I've got to be in a good headspace. I've got to be doing well. That drives me, too, because marriage isn't for everybody. But that's what's going to make *me* do it. That's what makes me happy. That's my definition of a happy marriage. My wife has helped me so much. Her presence really is the present.

Livin' the Life, Me and My Fine-Ass Wife

I'm an entertainer. This is my livelihood. I'm on the road constantly. My wife, she hosts parties and she has a big social media following. She has a fitness line and it's successful. She has makeup, wig, and accessory lines. Of course those are successful too. She's busy as hell. But I try to bring her with me as much as possible. I enjoy my life with my wife.

If I don't share my experiences with her, what's the use of having a wife? To me, it's the mature thing to do. I'll have problems at home if I don't bring her. Plus, if I'm gonna go somewhere and I don't bring my wife, why am I married? It don't make no sense, 'cause it's a choice. I married her to share these experiences with her and she's got her dreams too that she shares with me. It'd be selfish of me to not include her in what I'm doing, because I feel like I'm doing something special. We're privileged to have these times and it's good to celebrate them. So I feel like I would be denying her that.

I wouldn't respect myself for that and it would be obvious. Even if she didn't say something, I don't want to be that kind of guy and I don't want to have that type of wife. Even if she didn't say something and was okay with it, I don't even want to put that in her spirit. I want her to know that she's needed. Even if I didn't need her, I would say, "I need you to come. I want you to come." That's how I approach it. It's part of treating people how you want to be treated. Let's say she had more followers than anyone else in the world. I know she would bring me and include me, and make me feel important. I try to do the same thing for her.

She's shown me so much. She taught me a lot. A lot of stuff that I learned from her came from watching her. We started living together once I got out. We lived in my old house for a year and then we got married. The whole time I'd known her, she's one of the most consistent people I have ever known as far as saving her money, handling her business, running her business, how you talk to people, how you deal with people. Her spirit is a calm spirit. I envied that. At first, it was a challenge. I was jealous, like, "Damn. I wish that I had a demeanor where I don't just lose my temper. I wish that if somebody said something, I could choose not to get offended by it." I like to deal with them. If someone is being disrespectful, I could leave. That's what she does. She showed me another step of being grown and mature. Instead of choosing when I wanted to be acting grown, I felt like, "Okay, somebody did this," and I had permission to stoop to their level. She wouldn't do that. That challenged me to be more consistent, to be more adult about things. I'm watching her. She teaches me.

I hate to say it like this, but let's say you put two dogs together. One is a mean dog and the other has a cool temperament. One dog will adapt and the other will starve. That was me. I was around somebody who was so rational and calm and that was so by the book about not doing anything to compromise their money. She was very strategic about her business and living her life. She focused on getting the proper rest, the proper sleep. She separated her business from her friends. That started to affect me.

Once we really started to get to know each other and she knew my business, it was like, "Damn. She's got more money than I got. How did that happen? It shouldn't be like that. I'm supposed to have more money than she has." Yeah, I was in prison and hit rock bottom, but I'd spent all this money. She was like, "Damn. This is all the money you've got? I thought you had more." It was an embarrassing thing. I was like, "I was fortunate because I needed somebody to show me this, but this is what it's come to?" She was like, "Well, you've got to do better. Straight up."

Then it became a challenge. "If you get paid forty, fifty, sixty grand a show and I get ten grand for a party, you're not going to take into account what you're doing to pay the lawyer. I don't hang with all these people so I don't get these charges. That's stupid. Everything counts. We can't be like, 'if' or 'would' or 'could' have. If you don't commit any crimes, you know you'll have more money because you'll be blessed with a job where you get paid forty grand one time a week. If you think about it, that's 160 grand a month. Who's going to pay you that type of money?" She was breaking it down like that.

I was like, "Damn. I'm getting forty grand a week, 160 grand a month. If I would have just saved that money and paid the bills I had, I would have way more money than I've got. Where's the money been going?" Then it was like, "Okay. I can't get them years back, can't get the money back." Sometimes I was putting myself in deals where I wouldn't be getting money like that anymore. That's the reality of what it was. I couldn't be delusional. Same thing with my health. I had to decide what I was going to do. Was I going to keep eating, get fat as hell to where I get diabetes or die of a heart attack? Now it's not a secret. We're not in the days where you couldn't Google something to let you know, "This is going to kill you slowly."

Now I know better, so I do better. I have a lot to live for. I have the life I always dreamt of and a wife that's perfect for me.

Hot Wife, Rich Husband

Life is often about perception. Yeah, I've got a hot wife and I'm rich. That's the outside. But this book, it's about my thought process, how things work. That's why some of these words are about relationships, some are about money. This one is about both, and how they affect each other.

When money comes, it relieves stress. I'm not saying everything is about money. I grew up broke. But I always grew up around hardworking people. My mother worked the same job for thirty years. My brother worked a good-paying job, and he's probably been working there fifteen years. I feel like you're going to work for the quality of life you're going to get. I've seen that with people, even when I wasn't living that type of life. So I was like, "Why add a burden to myself when I have nothing?"

My wife wouldn't be a burden, but I've seen so many people where picking the right wife either makes you or breaks you. The choices you make show how smart you are. They show everything about you.

I wanted a wife who, not only did I love, but who could help me and who I could build something with, and who I'm proud to do things with. I wanted something that can last so that when I'm gone, I can pass something down. It ain't like back in the day when you just have kids for security, so that they can work the farm or so that when you're older the kids take care of you.

When I got married, I was thirty-seven years old. My wife and I have no kids together. It was a straight conscious choice. It was straight choice, not force.

My dad, on his side it's like ten or twelve of them. On my momma's side, it's like ten or twelve of them in Alabama. My granddaddy and my grandmom on both sides, they needed the kids. The kids brought income. Life was hard. The more kids you had, the more secure you were, the more hands you had to do whatever you needed to do, to run the business, help on the farm. Back then, cars were luxuries. Now, cars are a necessity and children are luxuries.

Think about things today. What happens if the more kids you have, the more it takes away from the money you have and it makes your quality of life go down? Times change and you've got to adapt and change.

But guess what? If you've got twelve kids, in today's times you probably don't have the money for that. It's not a luxury anymore to have that many kids. It inconveniences you in many ways. If you don't have the twelve kids, you have even more of an opportunity to go out and get the luxuries. That's the truth. If you don't do anything with the data, then you deserve your fate.

That's why it's about building brick by brick. I feel like make the money, then have a baby. We didn't come up like that, though. But

I'm like, "Hey, man. What did you think if we just did it like other people and just had enough money and then had a baby?" You've got to make sure the mother is healthy and that you have the resources to raise the baby right.

That takes money. So over the next two years, you save $1,000 a month. Then you take that twenty-four grand and you invest in real estate to make some money. Then you're like, "I watched this seminar and they told me I can give that twenty-four grand over and he's going to give me 30 percent interest for three years if I do that." If I had ten people I could tell to do that, guess what they've got to do? They've got to go to work every day.

They've got to take the bus in the rain. When their car is messed up, they've got to call their momma and say, "Hey, I know I messed up last time, but . . ." You see how this relationship has got to be cultivated? That is hard to do. I've seen my momma and my brother doing it. I know what it is to have to keep going to work. After four months, most people quit the job. They're like, "Man, that boss is trippin'. Man, I ain't gonna keep doing that stuff. Man, they're telling me I need to come in, do some more hours." There's so much stuff, so much humble pie that you've got to eat. There's so many things you can't do. You might have had a baby and have to give some of your check up. Now that you've met the one that you want, you think 'cause you had a child by somebody else that you don't have to take care of them, too.

You think she can't be jealous or be scorned? Do you think her being scorned gives you an excuse to not pay your taxes to where you're embarrassed and you might lose your business, your record label, your artists? All these things are reality for everybody.

The great self-help author Napoleon Hill said that picking a good wife is one of the smartest things you can do. He wrote the book *Think and Grow Rich*. Henry Ford and Abraham Lincoln had strong women behind them that drove them. I'm like, "Okay. That makes sense." He's showing me the data. He's telling me about all

these people who did all these successful things, and the people behind them. Then I'm like, "Okay. What makes this person different from me?" Only thing is he did the most with his time. I don't know when opportunities are going to come to me. I want to be great. Ford made the car. Lincoln became president, ended slavery, and saved the country. Another great idea might come next month and if I've got some money to invest, the next person who comes through, I might be part of that, especially if I'm in a good place in the community and they know me as a person with a following. It's possible if I leverage it, don't screw it up, and have some money. If I've got another job and I can bring artists to the table, that won't hurt anything.

I'm conscious of all these things. Let's say I have a clothing meeting. If I'm in good health and I go in to the meeting looking good, I'm pretty sure that's going to help me, too. So instead of just being the person to do the deal, I could wear the clothes, too. I could be a model and the executive. I could have been the CEO and been cool with that. There's nothing wrong with that. But now I can be a model, be in shape, and stand in front with it. That's more money, and I can live longer. That's just going to make the wife like you more, the people want to do business with you more. Why not adopt that? Why not get in on that, too?

The more beautiful I make my life, the more my wife is going to help me and drive me to even bigger and better success.

I'd Rather Just Chill Wit' Babe

I'm getting older. I'm forty years old. I'm a married person now. A wife or a husband or a soul mate—whoever you pick to live the rest of your life with—is one of the most important decisions you will ever make. It can make you or break you. Seriously. They're either going to be a liability or an asset. They're going to bring something to the table or take something from the table. And I'm not just saying this money-wise, even though two incomes are good. I'm blessed that my wife brings an income. Even if you were a farmer and your wife just cooked and fed you right to where you can go out there and make the most out of the farm, she held the house down to where you weren't sick. That would be important. But bring something to the table. Don't do things that are unhealthy to where I can't work, to where I'm stressed out and can't handle my business. I'm grateful I found the right wife. I'm grateful I found my soul mate. I love her. At this point in my life, I'd rather just chill with my baby.

Happy Wife, Happy Life

Put that in your pocket. Happy wife, happy life. It's catchy, and like many proverbs, it's simple. They're simple so you can teach them, so you can remember them. The truth is hard, but the truth is simple.

To enter into a marriage is a mutual agreement. There's certain things that you expect from your wife and certain things that she expects from you. Like anything, when everything's in perfect accord, things are good.

When you see that a marriage is in bad shape, it could be for a multitude of reasons. The wife may not be happy. The husband may not be happy. So whatever they're doing, whatever they agreed upon, it's rocky. It's unstable and it's causing heartache. So if you can't get to the point where your wife is happy, what are you doing? It ain't like it's one certain thing. I got some great advice that you don't have to get too high and you don't have to get too low. Just keep it where everything is going down the middle. Everybody in the house, the kids and anyone else, will be happy.

When everyone is happy, your wife is happy. When your wife is happy, you get that happy wife, happy life.

Part IX

Final Words

I'm Blessed and Grateful

I wrote that when I was coming back from Dubai at the top of 2020. Pop Smoke had just passed away. Kobe had just passed away. The coronavirus was breaking out, going throughout all parts of the world. I sat and looked at who I was, this life that I had. I'm blessed and I'm grateful. I got my health. I've got my beautiful wife. I've got a job that I'm still doing. I work hard for it. I have everything I need. I appreciate it. I want it to continue. I'm conscious that I've got to a lot to be grateful for.

People often forget those blessings that are right in front of them. It's the small things. You're either going to take care of it, or you're not going to take care of it. Something needs to get planted, so you're either going to plant and have whatever you wanted to grow, whatever you put in your garden. Or you're not going to plant anything and those weeds are going to grow in there. Either way, something's coming.

People can say that you don't have to watch what you eat. But guess what? Either you're going to put things into your body that are going to give you energy and make you feel better or you're going to do things that will make your days harder and more painful. It's as simple as that. The more you sit on your ass, the less energy you're going to have. That won't give you more. The more that you move around, the more energy you're going to have. Everybody knows that, or at least they should. Once you get that data and you don't do anything with it, hey man, that's on you. I operate from, "What can I do to push the envelope to make myself as healthy as possible?"

If I keep pushing myself with the idea of survival of the fittest, the idea of evolution, I'm evolving and helping everybody. If I invent something, or you invent something and it helps me, what are we doing? You're helping me. You're giving me the data and I do something with it and we make the next invention. We have been doing what historians and others have been doing for years. The only difference is that we're conscious of it. Was it fun doing it? Yes. Was it challenging? A little bit, yeah. As you do it more and more, did you find it rewarding? Yes. Yes, it is to me. That's how I work on my greatness every day.

Work hard on yourself always. But don't forget to stop, enjoy, appreciate, and be grateful for what you've achieved and where you're at.

Work hard on yourself always. But don't forget to stop, enjoy, appreciate, and be grateful for what you've achieved and where you're at.

If You Keep Looking Back, You'll Trip Going Forward

Not many rappers have gone from being damn near three hundred pounds to two hundred pounds. People always say, "What do you do health-wise?" I don't really show that stuff because I'm a rapper. I'm not a damn fitness trainer, but since you want to know, I'll tell you. I basically keep myself inspired to do what I gotta do because I'm not Kobe Bryant. I'm not an athlete. It's different with me. I want to show you how I grew up, and this is what I apply to my life. You can see that it's a living testimony. I have gone from unhealthy to healthy, from good to great. I reflect a lot in this book. But I keep my eyes on the present and the future. If you keep looking back, you'll trip going forward.

Never Quit on Yourself!

It's almost impossible to make someone believe in you if you don't believe in yourself. So never give up on yourself. Anything is possible. The world is watching. Don't give up. You've got greatness inside you.

Gucci Mane Acknowledgments

Thank you to my wife, Keyshia Ka'oir, for always being by my side. Thank you to the late Kobe Bryant for inspiring me to write this book.

Soren Baker Acknowledgments

Much of the success I have experienced in writing comes from the love, support, and inspiration provided by my parents, Alberta and Stanley Baker. They allowed me to embrace rap and dedicate virtually all of my free time (beginning at age 10) to consuming it, even though the music was foreign to them and had a largely negative rep. Thank you, Mom and Dad, for loving me and for supporting me in every step of my life.

Thank you, Grant Baker, for being a great brother, for all of your help with my writing, and for sharing my love of Ol' Dirty Bastard and Ludacris.

I've been blessed to have two phenomenal women in my day-to-day life in my adopted home of Southern California. My daughter, Loren, brings me immeasurable joy every day. Her intelligence and exuberance are two of the major motivating factors that push me every day. As you know, Loren, my love for you is infinite. DaVida Smith, thank you for blessing me with your love. You've become the best partner anyone could hope for. I love you.

Jorge Hinojosa, after you heard me on KDAY hosting Open Bar Radio with Xzibit, you gave me a call to reconnect and to ask me why I wasn't writing any of the major rap books hitting the market. Thanks to your belief in my ability as a writer, we began working together and I had the opportunity to write 2018's *The History Of Gangster Rap*.

Jorge's instincts proved correct when he suggested I connect with Robert Guinsler, a talented literary agent at Sterling Lord Literistic, Inc. Thank you, Robert, for believing in me and for suggesting that I write this book with Gucci Mane. Robert got me in touch with

243

Stuart Roberts, my editor at Simon & Schuster. Stuart, thank you for the opportunity and for working with me to make this book powerful.

Gucci Mane, thank you for the opportunity to work with you on this book. It's been a blessing.

Billy Johnson Jr., Shawndi Johnson, William "B-Luv" Taylor, Richie Abbott, Dave Weiner, Xzibit, Vidal Marsh, Kathy Iandoli, Steven Reissner, Daylan Williams, Ahmed Sabir-Calloway, Victoria Hernandez, Slink Johnson, J. Wells, James Kreisberg, Omar Burgess, Andres Tardio, Maurice Thomas, Valerie Sakmary, Andre Grant, Ural Garrett, Dana Dane, Chad Kiser, Leslie "Big Lez" Segar, and Amir Rahimi, thank you for your friendship and support.

Uncle Dion, Uncle Michael, Aunt Jo Anne, Uncle Paul, Aunt Linda, Aunt Mary Louise, Uncle Steve, Uncle Mark, Aunt Amy, Aunt Rosie, and Aunt Lois, thank you for your steady love and support.

Finally, thank you to the readers of this book. I appreciate your support.

Photo Credits

© Petra Collins: xvi, 63, 64–65, 116, 142

© Victor Demarchelier: 202

© Paras Griffin/Getty Images: 42

© Erik Madigan Heck/Trunk Archive: 151

© R Kikuo Johnson, originally published in *The New Yorker*: 238

© Jason Koerner/Getty Images: 120

© Cam Kirk: 80, 86, 188

© Quang Le: 108

© Matthew Marzahl: xii, xiv, 15, 20, 23, 30, 50, 54, 57, 73, 79, 88, 91, 92, 94, 102, 105, 110, 126, 129, 141, 146, 152, 155, 161, 166, 169, 170, 174, 176, 182, 194, 198, 201, 210, 214, 226, 232

© Cameron McCool: xx, 40

© Ryan McGinley: 144

© Johnny Nunez/Getty Images for BET: 98

© Simon Rasmussen: 124, 138

© Travis Shinn: 24, 29, 68

© John Spink/*Atlanta Journal-Constitution/Associated Press:* 236

© Gunner Stahl: 10, 34, 39

About the Authors

Gucci Mane is a critically acclaimed, platinum-selling recording artist, and *New York Times* bestselling author of *The Autobiography of Gucci Mane*. He has released fifteen studio albums and over a hundred overall projects. *The Gucci Mane Guide to Greatness* is his second book.

Soren Baker is the author of 2018's critically acclaimed *The History Of Gangster Rap*. Baker has written for the *New York Times*, *Los Angeles Times*, *XXL*, *The Source*, and the *Chicago Tribune*, among many others. He's penned liner notes for albums by 2Pac, Ice Cube, N.W.A, Gang Starr, and others, and has worked on television programs for VH1 and Fuse. His interviews appear on YouTube via his Unique Access Ent. channel.